The
Recreation Guide to Chicago & Suburbs

Chicago Review Press   820 N. Franklin Street, Chicago, IL 60610

© 1981 MUSEUM PUBLICATIONS OF AMERICA, INC., 10 South Wabash, Chicago, Illinois 60601, (312) 236-8724.

Produced by Steven L. Babecki. Edited by Warren L. Swanson. Written by Warren L. Swanson and Leonard F. Miska. Photography Steven R. Babecki.

ISBN 0-914090-65-8

TABLE OF CONTENTS

Introduction

This guide will introduce you to the great variety of recreational facilities available in your own back—or front—yard. It represents the most comprehensive list of Chicagoland recreational facilities ever compiled.

From the establishment of Dearborn Park in 1838, the Chicago Park District has expanded continually to meet the needs of a rapidly growing city. Today there are 576 parks in the system, and nearly 4,000 persons are employed full-time by the District to maintain and organize its myriad functions.

The Chicago Park District offers recreational activities for almost every interest. Both outdoor and indoor facilities for most popularly enjoyed sports are provided, as well as instruction programs and organized league play. Lessons in drama, music, and arts and crafts are also available through the District. The young, the elderly, and the handicapped are not neglected; programs designed for these special groups—such as day camps, senior citizen centers, and the Special Olympics—are prime examples of park services. Concerts in Grant Park and elsewhere help you relax after an exhausting day and—like virtually all the Park District programs—are free of charge.

Outside the city, the Cook County Forest Preserve District provides good fishing and boating waters, enough room for a number of winter sports, and thousands of acres of natural beauty. Recreation is the theme of the forest preserves, and various nature preserves around the Cook County area reveal what Illinois was like in its natural state.

For a glimpse into your past or an in-depth view of a favorite topic, you may wish to visit one of the many various museums in and around Chicago. All are free or quite inexpensive to visit; all are positively fascinating.

There is a world of enjoyment outside your own livingroom, a world free of membership fees and pretentious atmosphere. The Recreation Guide has been organized to help you enter it as easily as you can turn a page. Chapter One is an alphabetical listing of the recreational facilities available in Chicago area parks and forest preserves. If you are interested in a specific activity, Chapter One will tell you where you can find it. Then you can decide which location is most convenient or attractive to you by turning to the descriptions of individual parks in chapters 2, 3, 5 and 6. If you know the names of the parks near you, of course you can go directly to the individual listings in chapters 2, 3, 5 and 6. Chapter 4 describes special events and activities sponsored by the Chicago Park District, and chapter seven is a directory to museums in the area.

In short, the opportunities await you. All you need to take advantage of them is your own interest and this book.

A LISTING OF RECREATIONAL FACILITIES
IN CHICAGO AREA PARKS AND FOREST PRESERVES

This list covers most of the recreational facilities available in parks and forest preserves in and around Chicago. Where practical, specific locations are indicated. When locations are too numerous to list, information can be obtained by calling the appropriate park agency at the telephone numbers given below. A complete list of Park District numbers appears at the end of this chapter, p. 15.

Archery Ranges

12 at 10 locations:
Outdoor: Columbus, Lincoln (Belmont Harbor), Marquette, Riis, River, Washington
—with mound and target house: Columbus, Lincoln, Marquette, Riis
Indoor: Calumet, Columbus, Gage, Hamilton, Pulaski, Riis

Artcraft Instruction

92 locations; for information call 294-2320.

Art Gallery

Ridge; for information call 294-2320.

Art Centers

13 locations; for information call 294-2320.

Athletic Fields

185 at 162 locations; for information call 294-2492.

Baseball Diamonds

Senior: 171 at 106 locations
Junior: 307 at 156 locations
for information call 294-2325.

Basketball Backboards

1206 at 292 locations; for information call 294-2492.

Beach Houses

12 at 9 locations:
Calumet, Jackson, Foster Avenue, Leone, Montrose, North Avenue, 12th Street (Northerly Island), Rainbow, 31st Street. For information call 294-2333.

Bicycle Paths and Trails

31, plus Lakefront and channel paths. (The Lakefront path passes through Lincoln, Grant, Burnham, and Jackson Parks.)
Forest Preserve Bicycle Trails:
Arie Crown Forest (Salt Creek Division), I&M Canal (Palos Division), North Branch, Salt Creek, Thorn Creek

Bicycle Rental (privately owned and operated)

Diversey Harbor (East of Sheridan Road), Lincoln Park Zoo (across from refreshment stand), Olive Park/Navy Pier (Northeast corner, Ohio Street and North Outer Drive)
Hours: 10 a.m. to 7 p.m. daily
Rates:
$ 2.50/hour (one hour minimum)
$ 6.00/half day (3 hours)
$12.00/full day (8 hours)
Special family and group rates upon request.
Future sites: Waveland Park and Belmont Harbor

Boat Building Shops

Calumet, Harrison, Humboldt. For information call 294-2492.

Boating

Forest Preserves (general information, 261-8400 city, 366-9420, suburban)
Sailboating: E. J. Beck Lake, Big Bend Lake, Bode Lake, Busse Lake Des Plaines River, Powderhorn Lake, Skokie Lagoons
Canoeing: Beck Lake, Big Bend Lake, Busse Lake, Des Plaines River, Powderhorn Lake, Skokie

7

RECREATIONAL FACILITIES

Lagoons
Rowboat Rental: Busse Lake,
Maple Lake, Saganshkee Slough,
Tampier Lake
Rowboating (Private): Beck Lake,
Big Bend Lake, Busse Lake, Des
Plaines River, Powderhorn Lake,
Skokie Lagoons, Tampier
Lake
Motorboats: Des Plaines River
Boat Launch Ramps: Beck Lake,
Big Bend Lake, Busse Lake, Des
Plaines River, Skokie Lagoons

Bridle Paths
Burnham, Jackson, Lincoln,
Midway, Washington, No. 452

**Camera Clubs with
Darkroom Facilities**
Green Briar, Independence,
Lincoln, Portage, Ridge, River,
Washington

Casting Pools
Douglas, Garfield, Jackson,
Lincoln, Marquette, McKinley,
Riis, Sherman, Washington
With Pier: Jackson, Lincoln, Mar-
quette, Riis, Sherman

Ceramics
Athletic Field, Mt. Greenwood,
Portage, Ridge, Washington. For
information call 294-2320.

Children's Facilities
Playground Apparatus Areas: 493
at 435 locations
Sandboxes: 366 at 299 locations.
For information call 294-2492.

Club Rooms
873. located in Chicago Park
District Fieldhouses, Board of
Education Schools, Chicago
Housing Authority Commission

Center Buildings, and Chicago Park District Recreation Buildings.

Conservatories
Garfield, 300 N. Central Pk. Blvd. 533-1281
Lincoln, Fullerton & Stockton Dr., 294-4770

Craft Shops
Major Shops (with power tools): 47
Minor (part-time) Shops: 14
Glass-blowing: Athletic Field
For information call 294-2320.

Day Camps
165; for information call 294-2492.

Driving Ranges
Lincoln (Diversey): 8 a.m. to 10:45 p.m. daily
Forest Preserves: Pipe O'Peace and Highland Woods

Enameling
Austin Town Hall, Gage, Green Briar, Lincoln (Dickens), Ridge, Washington.

Fieldhouse Units
256; for information call 294-2492.

Football and Soccer Fields
204 at 157 locations; for information call 294-2492.

Golf Courses
Nine-hole: Columbus, Lincoln, Marquette, No. 429 (South Shore) ($3.00 fee; $3.50 weekends and holidays)

18-hole: Jackson ($4.00 fee; $4.50 weekends and holidays)
Senior citizens (65 and over) and Juniors (16 and under) are admitted for half price with identification permit from 5 a.m. to 5 p.m. daily and after 4 p.m. on weekends and holidays. Permits can be obtained from the Park District.

Forest Preserve Courses:
Nine-hole: Billy Caldwell (North Branch Division), Meadowlark (Salt Creek Division)
18-hole: "Chick" Evans (Skokie Division), Highland Woods, Edgebrook (North Branch Division), Indian Boundary (Indian Boundary Division), Pipe O'Peace and Burnham Woods (Calument Division)
Golf Carts Available: Highland Woods, "Chick" Evans, Indian Boundary, Pipe O'Peace, Burnham Woods ($10 fee per 18 holes)
Each course has a pro shop and refreshment stand. Children under 9 not allowed on courses. Children 9-12 must be accompanied by an adult.

Greens Fees:
Regular:
9-hole courses $3.00
18-hole courses $4.00
Highland Woods $5.00
Juniors (9-17) and Senior Citizens (65 and over);
9-hole courses $1.50
18-hole courses $2.00
Highland Woods $2.50
Juniors: Monday through Friday; no holidays. 10 a.m. to 3 p.m.

RECREATIONAL FACILITIES

Seniors: Monday through Friday; no holidays. Until 4 p.m.
I.D. cards available for Juniors and Seniors: $1.00 fee
Twilight Play: 18-hole course only; no holidays. After 4 p.m. $3.00 (Highland Woods $4.00)

Handball Courts
Outdoor: 23 at 13 locations
Indoor: Five at Pottawattomie, Washington, and West Lawn.
For information call 294-2492.

Harbors
Lincoln (Belmont, Montrose, Diversey), Burnham, Grant (Monroe), and Jackson (59th, Inner, Outer)
Marine Facilities (harbor hosts, slips, docks, moorings, sailing dinghy spaces): 3,539 at the above locations
Launching Ramps: Burnham, Jackson (59th Street), Lincoln (Diversey and Montrose), Calumet (at 95th Street), and Rainbow (at 79th Street)

Horseshoe Courts
310; for information call 294-2492.

Ice Skating Areas
Outdoor: 300
Indoor: California
For information call 294-2492.

Kitchens
152 at 134 locations; for information call 294-2492.

La Boccie Courts
13 at Armour Square, Blackhawk, Piotrowski, Shabbona, Riis, and Smith

Lagoons
17 at 15 locations; Boating Lagoon at Lincoln. For information call 294-2492.

Lagoon Fishing
Columbus, Douglas, Garfield, Humboldt, Jackson, Lincoln, Marquette, McKinley, Sherman, Washington

Lapidary Shops
Austin Town Hall, Gage, Green Briar, Jefferson, Lincoln (Administration Building), Ridge, Washington

Lawn Bowling
8 greens at 4 locations: Columbus, Jackson, Washington, No. 429 (South Shore)

Miniature Golf
18 holes: Lincoln (Diversey); 8 a.m. to 10:45 p.m. daily

Model Airplane Flying Fields
Forest Preserves: Palos, Calumet, Salt Creek, Indian Boundary

Model Trains
Calumet, Clarendon

Model Yacht Basins
Burnham (51st Street), Palmer

Multiple-Use Paved Areas
315; for information call 294-2492.

Music Instruction
45; for information call 294-2320.

Nature Centers
Forest Preserves: Little Red
Schoolhouse (Palos Division),
River Trail (Des Plaines Division),
Trailside Museum (Indian
Boundary Division), Sand Ridge
(Thorn Creek Division), Crabtree
(Northwest Division)

Outdoor Gardens
Lincoln (Rock, Main, and Grand-
mothers' Gardens), Grant (Rose

and Court of Presidents), Hum-
boldt, Douglas, Garfield (Formal
and Garden for the Blind),
Jackson, Marquette (Rose and
Trail Gardens), Washington,
Rainbow

Pianist Locations
47; for information call 294-2320.

Picnic Areas
166 at 131 locations; for information, call:
Illinois Department of Conservation: 793-2070
Nature Conservancy (666 North
Lake Shore Drive): 787-1791

RECREATIONAL FACILITIES

Play Camps
For younger children: 15. For information, call 294-2492.

Public Bath
Waller

Public Libraries
Hamilton, Sherman, Tuley

Rifle Range
Austin Town Hall

Senior Citizen Centers
54; for information call 294-2326.

Shuffleboard Courts
131 (Courts with sun canopy at Galewood and Rosenblum). For information call 294-2492.

Snowmobile Areas
Forest Preserves: 10 a.m. to 10 p.m.; $5 registration fee
North: Northwest Field (Northwest Division), Hintz Tract (Des Plaines Division), "Chick" Evans Golf Course, (Skokie Division)
Central: Indian Boundary Golf Course and Miller Meadow (Salt Creek Division), Morril Meadow (Palos Division)
South: Turtlehead Lake (Tinley Creek Division), Pipe O'Peace Golf Course (Calumet Division), North Creek Meadow (Thorn Creek Division)

Softball Diamonds
381; for information call 294-2492.

Special Activity and Historic Sites
Forest Preserves: Botanic Garden (Skokie Division), Brookfield Zoo and The Chicago Portage (Salt Creek Division)

Special Recreation Programs
(for mentally or physically handicapped)
11; for information call 294-2330.

Spray Pools
11; for information call 294-2492.

Stadia
Gately, Burnham (Soldier Field)

Swimming Facilities
294-2333
139 locations:
Major Beaches: 16
Minor Beaches: 15
Beaches with lockers and checking system: Calumet (South), Rainbow, Foster, Jackson (South), 31st Street, 12th Street, North Avenue, Montrose, Leone
For Beach Information, call 294-2333.
Swimming Lagoons: Humboldt, Douglas
Outdoor Pools: 72
Indoor Pools: 35
For information call 294-2333.
Forest Preserve Swimming Pools: Cermak Pool (Salt Creek Division), Whealan Pool (North Branch Division), Green Lake Pool (Thorn Creek Division)

Tennis Courts and Instruction
658 at 134 locations; for information call 294-2314.
Lighted: Waveland, Garfield, McKinley, Jackson, Tuley, Rainbow Beach, Lake Shore, Riis, Palmer, Beverly, River, Grant
Indoor: California (6)

SPECIAL ACTIVITIES

Citywide Tournament
In eight sections, from 12 and under to 45 and over
At Tuley, Riis, Beverly, Jackson, McKinley, Waveland, and Eugene Field

Entry fee: $1 (singles) and $2 (doubles) for children; $2 (singles) and $3 (doubles) for adults
Qualifying rounds: 1st or 2nd week of June
Finals: 1st or 2nd week of July

Junior Development Program
For children 18 and under
Tryouts are held in either the 2nd or 3rd week of June at Norwood, Riis, McKinley, Waveland, Mather, Marquette, and Tuley.
Youths selected will have weekly training sessions and be organized into teams for summer-long play

13

RECREATIONAL FACILITIES

U.S. Professional Tennis Association Program:
Two-hour clinics at McKinley
The clinics coincide with National Tennis Week, which is observed either the 2nd or 3rd week of June

Chicago Park District Tennis Association:
Adult league play: A, B, and C levels
Weekend mornings, beginning the first weekend of June

Outdoor Instruction:
At 40 to 50 locations
From mid-June until mid-August (7 to 8 weeks)

Indoor Instruction:
Beginning in April at various gymnasiums
Fees: $5 for adults; free for those under 17 and Senior Citizens

Toboggan Slides
Forest Preserves: Bemis Woods (Salt Creek Division), Dan Ryan Woods (Calumet Division), Deer Grove Slides, Jensen Slides (North Branch Division), Swallow Cliff Slides (Palos Division)

Tracks
Running: 26 (With Curb: Douglas, Dunbar, Jackson, Kilbourn, LaFollette, Lake Shore, Ogden, Riis)
Straight-away: 10

Trap-Shooting Range
Lincoln

Upholstery
Gage

Volleyball Courts
413 at 200 locations; for information call 294-2492.

Yoga Instruction
39 locations; $5 registration fee; for information call 294-2317.

Youth Group Camps
Forest Preserves: Des Plaines, Skokie, Thorn Creek (two sites), Tinley Creek (two sites)
By permit only.

Chicago Park District Information
(Administration Building, 425 E. McFetridge Dr., 294-2200)

Arts & Crafts 294-2320
Baseball 294-2325
Beach Information 294-2333
Concerts/Band Shell 294-2420
Drama Classes 294-2320
Golf Information 294-2274
Harbor Information 294-2270
Music 294-2320
Physical Activities 294-2316
Pool Information 294-2333
Public Information 294-2492
Senior Citizens Program 294-2326
Sewing Classes 294-2320
Special Recreation Program 294-2330
Swimming Classes 294-2333
Tennis Information 294-2314
Yoga Classes 294-2317

Conservatories
Garfield Park, 300 N. Central Pk. Blvd. 533-1281
Lincoln Park, Fullerton & Stockton Dr. 294-4770

Harbors
Belmont—Belmont Ave. & the Lake 281-8587
Burnham—1500 S. Linn White Dr. 294-4614
Diversey—Fullerton & the Lake 327-4430
59th Street—59th St. & the Lake 493-8704
Jackson—2200 E. 65th St. 363-6942
Monroe St.—Monroe & the Lake 294-4612
Montrose—Montrose & the Lake 878-3710
General Information: 425 E. McFetridge Dr., 294-2270

Park District-Owned Parking
East Monroe Underground
250 East Monroe 294-4740
Grant Park Underground
North—25 North Michigan Avenue 294-4598
South—325 South Michigan Avenue 294-4593
McCormick Place Underground
23rd and the Lake 294-4600
Soldier Field Lot
McFetridge Drive and South Lake Shore Drive 294-4593
General Information
425 East McFetridge Drive 294-2437

LAKEFRONT PARKS

Perhaps the best thing to happen to Lake Michigan since the founding of the City of Chicago is the system of parks embracing its western shore. The Chicago Lakefront is one extended park from East 79th Street (7900 south) to West Ardmore Avenue (5800 North), offering ample room for picnicking, swimming, sunbathing, boating, cycling, horseback riding, team sports, or just plain relaxing.

LINCOLN PARK
Chicago Academy of Science
Chicago Historical Society
Conservatory
Golf Course and Driving Range
Gun
Harbors—Belmont, Diversey,
Montrose
Theater on the Lake
Zoological Gardens

GRANT PARK
Art Institute
Buckingham Fountain
Monroe Street Harbor
James C. Petrillo Music Shell
Shedd Aquarium
The Field Museum of Natural
History
Underground Garage—North
Underground Garage—South

NORTHERLY ISLAND
Adler Planetarium
Merrill C. Meigs Airport
Rainbow Fleet (Burnham Harbor)

BURNHAM PARK
Burnham Harbor
Chicago Park District
Administration Building
McCormick Place
Soldier Field

JACKSON PARK
Golf Course
Harbors—Inner, Outer, 59th Street
Museum of Science and Industry

RAINBOW PARK
Marine Service Building

Major Attractions along the Lakefront

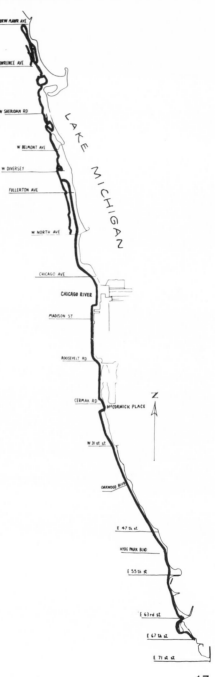

Lincoln Park
W. Armitage Ave. & N. Clark Sts.
& N. Lake Shore Dr. W. North Ave.
to W. Hollywood Ave.
(2000 N-231 W)
2045 N. Lincoln
294-4750

Margate Day Camp
4921 N. Marine
561-9809
Diversey Pool
606 E. Diversey
525-4460
Brauer Theater
2021 N. Stockton Dr.
294-4760
Conservatory
Fullerton & Stockton
294-4770
Fieldhouse
2045 N. Lincoln Pk. West
294-4750
—Boxing Program—294-4751
Zoo
2200 N. Cannon Dr.
294-4660

19

Lincoln Park

4 athletic fields, 5 baseball, 4 jr. baseball, 10 softball, 4 football & soccer, 33 tennis, 3 volleyball, 15 horseshoes, 5 shuffleboard, 11 basketball stds., 11 playgrounds, 2 spray pools, 6 sandboxes, 4 ice-skating, (North pond-1) (South pond-1) (Waveland-2), 2 day camps, bicycle path, bridle path, archery range, 7 bathing beaches, casting pool, golf course (9 hole), golf driving range, golf putting course, 3 yacht & powerboat harbors, 2 launching ramps, 1270 marine facilities, trap shooting range, zoo, 2 multiple-use paved areas, obstacle fitness course, 2 lagoons (1-boating, 1-fishing), fieldhouse (Margate), gymnasium, 2 clubrooms, kitchen, craft shop, senior citizen center, enameling, camera club, fieldhouse (Dickens), 3 clubrooms, lapidary shop, kitchen, art craft, music, enameling, pavilion (Fullerton), drama, kitchen, Cafe Brauer (Armitage), drama, 3 beach houses, yoga (Margate).

Grant Park

E. Randolph St. to E. McFetridge
Drive at Lake Michigan (150 N)

3 athletic fields, 2 jr. baseball, 18
softball, 4 football & soccer, 24
tennis, yacht & powerboat harbor,
900 marine facilities, ice rink.

Northerly Island Park
E. Roosevelt Rd. &
Lake Michigan (1200 S)

bathing beach, launching ramp,
beach house.

Burnham Park
(Includes East End & Promontory)
E. McFetridge Dr. to E. 56th St.
at Lake Michigan (1400 S)

Promontory

5491 S. Shore Dr.
324-2870

athletic field, baseball, 2 softball,
football & soccer, running track
(4 lap) (Soldier Field), 8 tennis, 3
multiple-use paved areas, 18
basketball stds., 2 volleyball, 6
playgrounds, spray pool, 2 sandboxes, ice-skating, bridle path,
bicycle path, 3 bathing beaches,
891 marine facilities, launching
ramp, model yacht basin, stadium
(Soldier Field), yacht & powerboat
harbor, day camp (promontory),
fieldhouse (promontory), 4 clubrooms, beach house.

Jackson Park
E. 63rd St. & S. Stony Island Ave.
(1600 E)
643-6363

3 athletic fields, 4 baseball, 10
softball, 5 football & soccer,
running track (4 lap), 24 tennis, 6
horseshoes, 4 volleyball, 2 bowling
greens, 11 basketball stds., 5 playgrounds, 5 sandboxes, bridle path,
bicycle path, day camp, 18 hole
golf course, launching ramp, 3
yacht & powerboat harbors, 478
marine facilities, 3 bathing
beaches, casting pool with pier,
2 multiple-use paved areas, fishing
lagoon, fieldhouse, gymnasium, 2
clubrooms, kitchen, drama, beach
house.

Rainbow Beach & Park

E. 75th to E. 79th St.
& Lake Michigan
734-5976

2 athletic fields, 2 jr. baseball, 3
softball, 2 football & soccer, 16
tennis, 3 handball, playground, 2
ice-skating, day camp, bathing
beach, launching ramp, 4 beach-
houses.

CITY CENTER PARKS

There is no need to despair if you don't live near Chicago's Lakefront; the city center parks offer many of the same facilities. Humboldt and Douglas parks have their own beaches along swimming lagoons, which certainly beats the problems caused by opening fire hydrants. Tennis enthusiasts can find courts scattered throughout the city, including indoor courts at California Park. A recent construction program has produced quite a number of modern fieldhouses—good places to stay in shape during the winter months. What follows is a summary of all the facilities of all the developed Chicago Park District properties. We think you'll be surprised by the recreational opportunities that are probably only a few blocks away from your home.

Abbott Park
9652 S. Michigan Ave. (100 E)
468-2411
Day Camp—49 E. 95th St.
264-1050

swimming pool, athletic field, 2 baseball, 3 jr. baseball, 2 football & soccer, running track (4 lap), 2 tennis, basketball stds., multiple-use paved area, 5 volleyball, 2 playgrounds, 2 spray pools, 2 sandboxes, 2 ice-skating, day camp, natatorium, 2 gymnasiums, assembly hall, 2 clubrooms, kitchen, drama, bathhouse.

Ada Park
11250 S. Ada St. (1326 W)
238-5255

swimming pool, athletic field, 2 baseball, 2 jr. baseball, softball, football & soccer, 4 tennis, horseshoes, multiple-use paved area, 4 volleyball, 4 basketball stds., play-

ground, spray pool, ice-skating, day camp, fieldhouse, gymnasium, combination assembly hall, 5 clubrooms, craft shop, kitchen, artcraft, senior citizen center.

Ada Playlot Park
715 S. Ada St. (1326 W)

playground, sandbox.

Adams Playground Park
1919 N. Seminary Ave. (1100 W)
472-5881

multiple-use paved area, 4 basketball stds., playground, sandbox, ice-skating, recreation building, 2 clubrooms.

Addams Park
1301 W. 14th St.

swimming pool, athletic field, baseball, junior baseball, 2 softball, football & soccer, multiple-use paved area, 4 basketball stds.,

28

volleyball, spray pool, gymnasium, combination assembly hall.

Albion Playlot Park
1752-68 W. Albion Ave. (6600 N)

multiple-use paved area, 2 basket-ball stds., playground, sandbox.

Altgeld Park
515 S. Washtenaw Ave. (2700 W)
638-0714

swimming pool, athletic field, baseball, 3 softball, football & soccer, multiple-use paved area, 2 basketball stds., volleyball, 4 shuffleboard, playground, spray pool, sandbox, ice-skating, day camp, fieldhouse, 2 gymnasiums, combination assembly hall, 2 club-rooms, kitchen, music.

Amundsen Park
6200 W. Bloomingdale Ave.
(1800 N)
637-7446

athletic field, 2 baseball, 2 jr. baseball, 5 softball, football & soccer, 2 multiple-use paved areas, 5 basketball stds., 5 volley-ball, playground, spray pool, ice-skating, day camp, fieldhouse, gymnasium, 7 clubrooms, craft shop, kitchen, artcraft, drama.

Anderson Playground Park
3748 S. Prairie Ave. (300 E)
373-1136

multiple-use paved area, 4 basket-ball stds., playground, ice-skating, spray pool, recreation building, 2 clubrooms.

Archer Park
4901 S. Kilbourn Ave. (4500 W)
735-5080

athletic field, baseball, 2 jr. baseball, 2 softball, football & soccer, 2 tennis, multiple-use paved area, 4 basketball stds., 4 volleyball, playground, sandbox, 2 ice-skating, day camp, spray pool, 3 horseshoes, fieldhouse, gymnasium, 44 clubrooms, craft shop, kitchen, recreation building, clubroom, artcraft.

Armour Square Park
3309 S. Shields Ave. (332 W)
294-4732

swimming pool, athletic field, baseball, 3 softball, football & soccer, 3 tennis, 2 la bocci, 2 volleyball, 2 horseshoes, 2 hand-ball, 4 shuffleboard, 6 basketball stds., playground, spray pool, 2 sandboxes, ice-skating, day camp, multiple-use paved area, field-house, 2 gymnasiums, assembly hall, 5 clubrooms.

Arrigo Park
W. Lexington St. & S. Lytle St. (1250 W & 800 S)

2 jr. baseball.

Ash Playlot Park
501-31 W. Wisconsin St. (1900 N)

4 basketball stds., playground, ice-skating.

Ashland Playlot Park
5233 N. Ashland Ave. (1600 W)

playground, sandbox.

Aspen Playlot Park
4237-41 W. Wabash Ave. (45 E)

playground.

Aster Playlot Park
4639 N. Kenmore Ave. (1040 W)

playground, sandbox, spray pool.

Athletic Field Park
3546 W. Addison St. (3600 N)
588-5556
Pottery Studio—
3623 N. Central Park
267-6294

athletic field, 4 softball, football & soccer, 4 tennis, 4 horseshoes, multiple-use paved area, 3 basketball stds., 3 volleyball, playground, spray pool, sandbox, 2 ice-skating, day camp, fieldhouse, 7 clubrooms, kitchen, artcraft, ceramics, glassblowing, music.

Auburn Park
406 W. Winneconna Parkway (7800 S)

passive recreation area, lagoon, ice-skating.

Augusta Playground Park
4431 W. Augusta Blvd. (1000 N)
235-8484

jr. baseball, multiple-use paved area, playground, sandbox, ice-skating, 2 basketball stds., volley-ball, recreation building, clubroom.

Austin Park
5951 W. Lake St. (200 N)

swimming pool, spray pool, play-ground, bathhouse.

Austin Town Hall Park
5610 W. Lake St. (200 N)
378-0126

multiple-use paved area, 2 basket-ball stds., volleyball, day camp, special recreation program, field-house, natatorium, gymnasium, assembly hall, 8 clubrooms, 3 kitchens, lapidary shop, enameling, rifle range.

Avalon Park
1215 E. 83rd St.
734-8139

swimming pool, 2 athletic fields, baseball, jr. baseball, 6 softball, 2 football & soccer, running track (6 lap), 6 tennis, 6 horseshoes, 4 shuffleboards, 3 multiple-use paved areas, 5 basketball stds., 2 volleyball, playground, spray pool, sandbox, 2 ice-skating, day camp, fieldhouse, gymnasium, 4 club-rooms, craft shop, kitchen, drama, music, senior citizen center, yoga.

Avenue "L" Playlot Park
10556-58 S. Avenue L (3600 E)

playground, sandbox, spray pool.

Avenue M Playlot Park
13401-11 S. Avenue M (3532 E)

multiple-use paved area, 2 basket-ball, stds., playground, sandbox.

Avondale Park
3516 W. School St. (3300 N)
463-3729

swimming pool, multiple-use paved area, 2 basketball stds., volleyball, playground, spray pool, sandbox, day camp, fieldhouse, gymnasium, assembly hall, 8 club-rooms, craft shop, 2 kitchens, artcraft, drama, music, art center, yoga.

Baraga Playlot Park
2434-44 S. Leavitt St. (2200 W)

playground, 2 basketball stds., sandbox.

Barberry Playlot Park
2825-27 W. Arthington St. (900 S)

playground, spray pool, sandbox.

Barnard Playground Park
10431-59 S. Longwood Drive
(1800 W)

playground, spray pool, sandbox, ice-skating.

Barrett Playground Park
2022 W. Cermak Rd. (2200 S)
294-4706

2 basketball stds., playground, ice-skating, recreation building, clubroom.

Bauler Playlot Park
2000-16 N. Burling St. (732 W)

multiple-use paved area, 2 basket-ball stds., playground, sandbox.

Beech Playlot Park
4458-70 S. Oakenwald Ave. (1100 E)

playground, spray pool.

Beilfuss (Natatorium) Park
1725 N. Springfield Ave. (3900 W)
235-0282

jr. baseball, playground, natatorium building.

Bell Park
3020 N. Oak Park Ave. (6800 W)
889-2114

jr. baseball, softball, 2 tennis, 3 horseshoes, 2 multiple-use paved areas, 4 basketball stds., 2 volley-ball, playground, spray pool, sand-box, 2 ice-skating, day camp, fieldhouse, 3 clubrooms, kitchen.

Bell Playlot Park
819 S. Bell Ave. (2234 W)

playground.

CITY CENTER PARKS

Bensley Park
9729 S. Yates Ave. (2400 E)
734-6441

athletic field, 2 jr. baseball, football & soccer, multiple-use paved area, 2 volleyball, 2 basketball stds., playground, sandbox, ice-skating, day camp, 2 tennis, recreation building, clubroom, kitchen.

Bessemer Park
8930 S. Muskegon Ave. (2838 E)
768-1079

swimming pool, athletic field, 2 baseball, 4 softball, football & soccer, running track (5 lap), 6 tennis, 2 handball, 5 horseshoes, 4 shuffleboard, multiple-use paved area, 4 basketball stds., volleyball, playground, spray pool, 3 sandboxes, 2 ice-skating, bicycle path, day camp, fieldhouse, 2 gymnasiums, assembly hall, 6 clubrooms, kitchen.

Beverly Park
2460 W. 102nd St.
776-4441

athletic field, baseball, 3 softball, football & soccer, 4 tennis, 4 horseshoes, 2 shuffleboard, 2 multiple-use paved areas, 4 basketball stds., 2 volleyball, playground, ice-skating, day camp, sandbox, spray pool, recreation building, clubroom.

Birch Playlot Park
425-29 E. 45th St.

playground.

Bixler Playlot Park
5641-59 S. Kenwood Ave. (1332 E)

playground, spray pool, sandbox.

Blackhawk Park
2318 N. Lavergne Ave. (5000 W)
237-3877

athletic field, 3 softball, football & soccer, 5 tennis, 2 multiple-use paved areas, 8 basketball stds., 2 volleyball, playground, spray pool, sandbox, ice-skating, day camp, 2 la bocci, special recreation program, fieldhouse, natatorium, gymnasium, assembly hall, 9 clubrooms, craft shop, kitchen, artcraft, senior citizen center.

Block (Griffith Natatorium) Park
346 W. 104th St.

2 basketball stds., natatorium building.

Bogan Park
3939 W. 79th St.
582-4464

athletic field, baseball, jr. baseball, 2 softball, football & soccer, straight-away tract (1 lap), 2 tennis, multiple-use paved area, 4 basketball stds., 4 volleyball, playground, ice-skating, day camp, natatorium, 2 gymnasiums, assembly hall, 3 clubrooms, art-craft, music, recreation building, clubroom, drama.

Bosley Playground Park
3044 S. Bonfield St. (1300 W)
294-4707

softball, 2 horseshoes, multiple-use paved areas, 2 basketball stds., playground, spray pool, ice-skating, volleyball, recreation building, 2 clubrooms.

Brainerd Park
1246 W. 92nd St.
233-6090

athletic field, 2 baseball, 2 jr. baseball, 2 softball, football & soccer, 5 tennis, 2 volleyball, 2 shuffleboard, 8 basketball stds., playground, spray pool, sandbox, 2 ice-skating, day camp, multiple-use paved area, fieldhouse, gymnasium, 3 clubrooms, kitchen, artcraft, drama.

Brands Park
3285 N. Elston Ave. (2900 W)
463-3759

softball, 2 tennis, volleyball, 5 horseshoes, 4 basketball stds., 2 playgrounds, spray pool, 2 sand-boxes, ice-skating, day camp, fieldhouse, gymnasium, 5 club-rooms, kitchen, music, craft shop.

Brooks Park
7100 N. Octavia Ave. (7300 W)
774-3404

athletic field, 3 jur. baseball, football & soccer, straightaway track (1 lap), 2 tennis, volleyball, 6 horseshoes, 4 basketball stds., playground, spray pool, 2 sandboxes, 2 ice-skating, day camp, fieldhouse, 3 clubrooms, kitchen.

Buckeye Playlot Park
W. Ainslie St. & N. Troy St.
(4900 N & 3132 W)

playground, sandbox.

Buckthorn Playlot Park
4345-49 S. Calumet Ave. (344 E)

4 basketball stds., playground, volleyball.

Buena Playlot Park
W. Buena and N. Kenmore Ave.
(4200 N & 1040 W)

swimming pool, playground.

Buttercup Playlot Park
4901-23 N. Sheridan Rd. (400 W)

playground, sandbox.

Butternut Playlot Park
5324 S. Woodlawn Ave. (1200 E)

playground, sandbox.

California Park
3834 N. California Ave. (2800 W)
478-0953

swimming pool, softball, 4 tennis, 5 volleyball, 4 shuffleboard, multiple-use paved area, 4 basketball stds., playground, sandbox, wading pool, day camp.

Wm. L. McFetridge Sports Center
3845 N. California Ave.
478-0210

indoor ice-skating arena, 6 indoor tennis.

Calumet Parkway Park
6210 S. Calumet Ave. (344 E)

swimming pool, passive recreation area.

Carmen Playlot Park
1224 W. Carmen Ave. (1500 N)

playground, sandbox.

Carpenter Playlot Park
6153-57 S. Carpenter St. (1032 W)

playground.

Caruso Playlot Park
301-25 W. 26th St.

playground, spray pool, sandbox.

Carver Park
939 E. 132nd St.
928-6555

athletic field, 2 baseball, jr. baseball, 6 softball, 2 football & soccer, straightaway track (1 lap), multiple-use paved area, 8 basketball stds., volleyball, ice-skating, day camp, combination gymnasium/assembly hall, 2 clubrooms, craft shop, kitchen, music, natatorium.

Catalpa Playlot Park
4324-36 S. Kedvale Ave. (4134 W)

playground, spray pool, sandbox.

Cedar Playlot Park
5311-17 N. Winthrop Ave. (1100 W)

multiple-use paved area, 2 basketball stds., playground, spray pool, sandbox.

Central Playlot Park
721 N. Central Park Ave. (3600 W)

playground, sandbox.

Chase Park
4701 N. Ashland Ave. (1600 W)
561-4887

swimming pool, athletic field, 3 softball, football & soccer, running track (5 lap), 4 tennis, volleyball, 5 horseshoes, multiple-use paved area, 6 basketball stds., ice-skating, day camp, fieldhouse, gymnasium, 5 clubrooms, craft shop, kitchen, drama, yoga.

CITY CENTER PARKS

Cherry Playlot Park
4611-19 N. Racine Ave. (1200 W)

passive recreation area,
chess/checker tables.

Chestnut Playlot Park
7001-09 S. Dante Ave. (1432 E)

multiple-use paved area, 2 basketball stds., playground, sandbox.

Chippewa Park
6785 N. Sacramento Ave. (3000 W)
274-4288

multiple-use paved area, 4 basketball stds., playground, spray pool,
sandbox, ice-skating, day camp,
fieldhouse, 5 clubrooms, kitchen,
artcraft, art center.

Chokeberry Playlot Park
6644-48 S. University Ave. (1144 E)

playground, 8 basketball stds.,
volleyball.

Chopin Park
3420 N. Long Ave. (5400 W)
283-3418

athletic field, baseball, 2 jr.
baseball, football & soccer, 4
tennis, 4 horseshoes, 2 volleyball,
2 basketball stds., playground,
spray pool, 2 ice-skating, day
camp, fieldhouse, assembly hall, 8
clubrooms, 2 kitchens, drama,
senior citizen center, yoga.

Christiana Playlot Park
1533 S. Christiana Ave. (3332 W)

playground, sandbox, basketball
std.

Claremont Playlot Park
2324-58 W. Flournot St. (700 S)

multiple-use paved area, 4 basketball stds., playground, sandbox.

Clarendon Community Center Park
4501 N. Clarendon Ave. (800 W)
561-1274

athletic field, jr. baseball, 3 softball, football & soccer, multiple-use paved area, 3 basketball stds., volleyball, playground, ice-skating, day camp, chess/checker tables, recreation building, 2 clubrooms.

Clark Playground Park
4615 W. Jackson Blvd. (300 S)
626-8326

swimming pool, athletic field, 2 softball, football & soccer, multiple-use paved area, 3 basketball stds., volleyball, playground, ice-skating, day camp, chess/checker tables, recreation building, 2 clubrooms.

Clover Playlot Park
2210 N. Southport Ave. (1400 W)

multiple-use paved area, 2 basketball stds., playground, sandbox.

Clybourn Playlot Park
1755 N. Clybourn Ave. (932 W)

multiple-use paved area, 2 basketball stds., playground, sandbox.

Cole Park
361 E. 85th St.
874-9665

2 jr. baseball, multiple-use paved area, 6 basketball stds., volleyball, playground, spray pool, sandbox, ice-skating, day camp, recreation building, clubroom, kitchen, artcraft.

Columbus Park
500 S. Central Ave. (5600 W)
378-0643

swimming pool, 2 athletic fields, 2 baseball, 3 jr. baseball, 2 softball, 2 football & soccer, 9 tennis, 3 horseshoes, multiple-use paved area, 4 basketball stds., 2 volleyball, 2 playgrounds, spray pool, wading pool, sandbox, archery range, 2 bowling greens, nine-hole golf course, bicycle path, 2 ice-skating, day camp, fishing lagoon, fieldhouse, 2 gymnasiums, 2 assembly halls, 10 clubrooms, craft shop, 2 kitchens, artcraft, archery range, music, senior citizen center.

Commercial Park
1845 W. Rice St. (832 N)
294-4704

jr. baseball, multiple-use paved area, 2 basketball stds., playground, sandbox, ice-skating, day camp, fieldhouse, gymnasium, 2 clubrooms.

CITY CENTER PARKS

Cooper Park
W. 117th St. & S. Ada St. (1332 W)

2 jr. baseball, multiple-use paved area, 4 basketball stds., playground, sandbox, ice-skating, day camp (play camp), recreation building, clubroom, kitchen.

Cornell Park
5473 S. Cornell Ave. (1632 E)

playground, sandbox.

Cornell Square Park
1809 W. 50th St. (5010 S. Wood St.)
776-1099

swimming pool, athletic field, baseball, 2 jr. baseball, football & soccer, 3 tennis, multiple-use paved area, 4 basketball stds., 4 volleyball, playground, spray pool, sandbox, ice-skating, day camp, fieldhouse, 2 gymnasiums, assembly hall, 5 clubrooms, craft shop, kitchen, artcraft, drama.

Cragin Playground Park
2611 N. Lockwood Ave. (5300 W)
622-0106

athletic field, 2 jr. baseball, football & soccer, 4 tennis, multiple-use paved areas, 4 basketball stds., volleyball, playground, sandbox, 2 ice-skating, day camp, recreation building, clubroom.

Cranberry Playlot Park
4315 N. Kenmore Ave. (1040 W)

playground, sandbox.

Crescent Park
2200-58 W. 108th Pl.

athletic field, softball, football & soccer, 2 tennis, 2 basketball stds., ice-skating, playground.

Daisy Playlot Park
2230 W. Cortland St. (1900 N)

playground, sandbox.

Dauphin Park
8701-8859 & 9015 S. Dauphin Ave. (889 E)

passive recreation area, playground.

Davis Playlot Park
5427 W. Division St. (1200 N)

multiple-use paved area, 2 basketball stds., playground.

Davis Square Park
4430 S. Marshfield (1632 W)
927-1983

swimming pool, athletic field, 2 softball, football & soccer, 4 tennis, 4 volleyball, 4 horseshoes, multiple-use paved area, 4 basketball stds., playground, spray pool, 2 sandboxes, ice-skating, day camp, fieldhouse, 2 gymnasiums, assembly hall, 5 clubrooms.

Dawes Park
8052 S. Damen Ave. (2000 W)
846-4950

athletic field, baseball, 3 jr. baseball, softball, football & soccer, multiple-use paved area, 4 basketball stds., volleyball, playground, spray pool, ice-skating, straightaway track, day camp, recreation building, clubroom, kitchen.

Dean Playground Park
1344-68 N. Dean St. (1700 W)
384-1850

softball, multiple-use paved area, 5 basketball stds., volleyball, playground, spray pool, sandbox, ice-skating, recreation building, clubroom.

De George Playlot Park
4901-09 W. Wabansia Ave. (1700 N)

playground.

De Julio Playlot Park
6056 N. Landers Ave. (5100 W)

playground, spray pool, sandbox.

Dickinson Playground Park
4101-31 N. Lavergne Ave. (5000 W)

playground, spray pool.

Dobson Playlot Park
7521-31 S. Dobson Ave. (1032 E)

playground, sandbox.

Dogwood Playlot Park
2732-36 W. Polk St. (800 S)

playground.

Donovan Playground Park
3620 S. Lituanica Ave. (900 W)
523-7522

athletic field, baseball, jr. baseball, football & soccer, multiple-
use paved area, 2 basketball stds.,
volleyball, playground, ice-
skating, spray pool, day camp,
recreation building, clubroom.

Dooley Playground Park
3402-48 W. 77th St.

jr. baseball, multiple-use paved
area, 4 basketball stds., volleyball,
playground, sandbox, ice-
skating.

Dougherty Playground Park
9314-56 S. Kingston Ave. (2532 E)

athletic field, baseball, jr. league.

Douglas Park
W. 14th St. & S. Albany Ave.
(3100 W)
521-3244

swimming lagoon, swimming
pool, athletic field, 3 baseball, 2 jr.
baseball, 4 football & soccer,
running track (4 lap), 5
multiple-use paved areas, 20
basketball stds., 2 volleyball, 4

horseshoes, 5 playgrounds, 2
spray pools, 2 sandboxes, bicycle
path, casting pool, day camp,
special recreation program, fishing
lagoon, fieldhouse, 2
gymnasiums, combination
assembly hall, 7 clubrooms,
kitchen, art craft.

Dubkin Playlot Park
7442 N. Ashland Ave. (1600 W)

sandbox.

Dunbar Park
3000 S. King Drive (400 E)
294-4695

athletic field, 2 baseball, 2 jr.
baseball, 2 football & soccer, 2
multiple-use paved areas, 8
basketball stds., 8 volleyball,
4 tennis, running track (4 lap), 2
playgrounds, 2 sandboxes, ice-
skating, day camp, natatorium, 2
gymnasiums, assembly hall, 5
clubrooms, kitchen, music.

Dunham Park
4640 N. Melvina Ave. (6200 W)
283-1168

athletic field, baseball, 4 jr. baseball, 3 tennis, 2 horseshoes,
multiple-use paved area, 4 basketball stds., volleyball, playground,
sandbox, 2 ice-skating, day camp,
spray pool, fieldhouse,
gymnasium, 3 clubrooms, craft
shop, kitchen, artcraft, yoga.

Durkin Park
8441 S. Kolin Ave. (4332 W)
767-7667

athletic field, baseball, 2 jr.
baseball, softball, 2 football &
soccer, multiple-use paved area, 4
basketball stds., 4 volleyball, playground, spray pool, sandbox, 2
ice-
ice-skating, day camp, play camp,
gymnasium, combination
assembly hall, 5 clubrooms, artcraft, drama.

Dvorak Park
1119 W. Cullerton St. (2000 S)
294-4708

swimming pool, athletic field, jr.
baseball, 2 softball, football &
soccer, shuffleboard, 3 horseshoes, multiple-use paved area, 2
basketball stds., volleyball, 2 playgrounds, spray pool, ice-skating,
sandbox, fieldhouse, 2 gymnasiums, combination assembly
hall, 5 clubrooms, craft shop,
kitchen.

Eckersall Playground Park
2400-58 E. 82nd St.

2 multiple-use paved areas, 5
basketball stds., playground, ice-
skating, volleyball.

Eckhart Park
1330 W. Chicago Ave. (800 N)
294-4710

athletic field, 3 baseball, football & soccer, multiple-use paved area, 4 basketball stds., volleyball, playground, sandbox, ice-skating, day camp, special recreation program, fieldhouse, natatorium, 2 gymnasiums, combination assembly hall, 6 clubrooms, craft shop, kitchen.

Edgebrook Playlot Park
6500-24 N. Algonquin Ave. (5500 (5500 W)

multiple-use paved area, 2 basketball stds., playground, sandbox.

Edison Park
6755 Northwest Highway (7600 W)
631-3471

playground, day camp, fieldhouse, 6 clubrooms, kitchen, senior citizen center.

Elder Playlot Park
1862-66 S. Avers Ave. (3832 W)

playground.

Eleanor Playlot Park
2731-41 S. Eleanor St. (1400 W)

playground, sandbox.

Ellis Park
707 E. 37th St.
548-4661

athletic field, 3 jr. baseball, football & soccer, 2 tennis, multiple-use paved area, 4 basket-

ball stds., volleyball, straightaway track (1 lap), playground, spray pool, sandbox, day camp, gymnasium, assembly hall, 5 clubrooms, craft shop, drama, kitchen, artcraft, music.

Elm Playlot Park
5215 S. Woodlawn Ave. (1200 E)

sandbox.

Elston Playlot Park
3451-69 N. Troy St. (3132 W)

multiple-use paved area, basketball std., playground, spray pool, sandbox.

Emerald Playlot Park
5600 S. Emerald Ave. (732 W)

2 basketball stds.

Emmerson Playground Park
1820 W. Granville Ave. (6200 N)
743-3170

2 tennis, 6 basketball stds., playground, spray pool, sandbox, 2 ice-skating, multiple-use paved area, recreation building, clubroom.

Euclid Park
9701-9833 S. Wallace St. (600 W)
238-0857

athletic field, 2 jr. baseball, football & soccer, 2 tennis, multiple-use paved area, 4 basketball stds., 4 volleyball, playground, spray pool, sandbox, ice-skating, day camp, recreation building, clubroom, kitchen, art-craft.

Eugene Field Park
5100 N. Ridgeway Ave. (3732 W)
478-1210

athletic field, baseball, 2 softball, football & soccer, 5 tennis, 2 volleyball, horseshoes, multiple-use paved area, 5 basketball stds., playground, spray pool, 2 sand-boxes, 2 ice-skating, day camp, fieldhouse, gymnasium, assembly hall, 12 clubrooms, craft shop, kitchen, drama, senior citizen center.

Evergreen Playlot Park
631 W. Belmont Ave. (3200 N)

multiple-use paved area, 2 basket-ball stds., playground.

Ewing Playlot Park
9812-14 S. Ewing Ave. (3634 E)

playground, spray pool, sandbox.

Fellger Playlot Park
2000-24 W. Belmont Ave. (3200 N)

playground, sandbox.

Fernwood Park
10438 S. Lowe Ave. (632 W)
238-7653

athletic field, baseball, 2 jr. base-ball, football & soccer, 6 tennis,

4 horseshoes, 4 shuffleboard, multiple-use paved area, 4 basketball stds., 4 volleyball, playground, spray pool, sandbox, 2 ice-skating, day camp, fieldhouse, 4 clubrooms, kitchen.

Filbert Playlot Park
1822 W. Larchmont Ave. (3932 N)

playground, sandbox.

Forest Glen Playlot Park
5069-77 W. Berwyn Ave. (5300 N)

playground, sandbox

Fosco Playground Park
1313 S. Throop St. (1300 W)
294-4709

2 softball, 2 multiple-use paved areas, 4 basketball stds., volleyball, playground, 2 ice-skating, clubroom, kitchen.

Foster Park
1440 W. 84th St.
723-7215

athletic field, 2 baseball, jr. baseball, 3 softball, football & soccer, running track (6 lap), 8 tennis, 4 horseshoes, 3 multiple-use paved areas, 3 volleyball, 4 shuffleboard, 10 basketball stds., playground, spray pool, 3 sandboxes, 2 ice-skating, day camp, fieldhouse, natatorium, 2 gymnasiums, combination assembly hall, 6 clubrooms, craft shop, 2 kitchens, art-craft, drama, music, senior citizen center.

Franklin Park
1449 S. Kolin Ave. (4332 W)
521-2306

swimming pool, athletic field, baseball, 3 softball, football & soccer, multiple-use paved area, 8 basketball stds., ice-skating, day camp, playground, fieldhouse, gymnasium, 4 clubrooms, craft shop, kitchen.

Fuller Park
331 W. 45th St.
268-0062

swimming pool, athletic field, baseball, 2 softball, football & soccer, 2 tennis, 2 horseshoes, multiple-use paved area, 6 basketball stds., 2 volleyball, playground, spray pool, 3 sandboxes, ice-skating, day camp, fieldhouse, 2 gymnasiums, assembly hall, 10 clubrooms, craft shop, kitchen, artcraft, drama, senior citizen center.

Fulton Playlot Park
4626 Fulton St. (300 N)

playground, spray pool, sandbox.

Gage Park
2415 W. 55th St.
434-6393

swimming pool, 2 athletic fields,

3 baseball, 2 jr. baseball, 5 softball, football & soccer, running track (6 lap), 2 multiple-use paved areas, 4 shuffleboard, 4 basketball stds., 2 volleyball, playground, spray pool, 2 sandboxes, 2 ice-skating, 5 horseshoes, day camp, 2 handball, tennis, special recreation program, fieldhouse, 2 gymnasiums, assembly hall, 14 clubrooms, craft shop, 2 kitchens, lapidary shop, archery range, music, enameling, senior citizen center, upholstery.

Galewood Playground Park
5729 W. Bloomingdale Ave. (1800 N)
622-3877

2 softball, 2 tennis, 2 horseshoes, 7 shuffleboard, multiple-use paved area, 6 basketball stds., 4 volleyball, playground, spray pool, sandbox, 2 ice-skating, day camp, recreation building, clubroom.

Gately Park
810 E. 103rd St.
928-6160

2 athletic fields, baseball, 2 jr. baseball, 4 softball, 2 football & soccer, stadium, 2 multiple-use paved areas, 5 volleyball, 8 basketball stds., playground, sandbox, 2 ice-skating, day camp, recreation building, clubroom.

Gill Park
825 W. Sheridan Rd. (3900 N)
525-7238

2 horseshoes, 3 shuffleboard, playground, day camp, special recreation program, fieldhouse, natatorium, gymnasium, assembly hall, 6 clubrooms, craft shop, kitchen, artcraft, yoga.

47

CITY CENTER PARKS

Ginkgo Playlot Park
W. 15th & S. Trumbull Ave. (3432 W)

playground.

Gladstone Park
5421 N. Menard Ave. (5800 W)
763-8338

softball, horseshoes, basketball std., playground, sandbox, ice-skating, day camp, spray pool, fieldhouse, 2 clubrooms, kitchen, music.

Gladys Playlot Park
3301-11 W. Gladys Ave. (332 S)

multiple-use paved area, 2 basketball stds., playground, spray pool, sandbox.

Goldberg Playlot Park
7043-61 N. Glenwood Ave. (1400 W)

Golden Gate Park
E 130th St. & S. Eberhart Ave. (500 E)

2 jr. baseball, multiple-use paved area, 4 basketball stds., playground, spray pool, sandbox.

Goldenrod Playlot Park
N Wood St. & N. Avondale Ave. (1800 W & 2030 N)

playground, 2 sandboxes.

Gompers Park
4222 W. Foster Ave. (5200 N)
736-4338

swimming pool, athletic field, 3 jr. baseball, football & soccer, 6 tennis, 2 multiple-use paved areas, 3 volleyball, 6 basketball stds., playground, spray pool, sandbox, 2 ice-skating, lagoon, day camp, fieldhouse, gymnasium, assembly hall, 5 clubrooms, 2 kitchens, art-craft, drama.

Gooseberry Playlot Park
4648 N. Malden St. (1300 W)

playground, sandbox.

Goudy Square Playlot Park
1249-61 N. Astor St. (50 E)

playground, sandbox.

Grand Crossing Park
7655 S. Ingleside Ave. (932 E)
723-3262

swimming pool, athletic field, 2 baseball, 5 softball, football & soccer, running track (6 lap), 6 tennis, 2 volleyball, 5 horseshoes, multiple-use paved area, 4 basketball stds., playground, spray pool, 3 sandboxes, 2 ice-skating, day camp, fieldhouse, 2 gymnasiums, combination assembly hall, 7 clubrooms, craft shop, artcraft, senior citizen center.

Grand Playlot Park
3529-33 W. Grand Ave. (1100 N)

playground.

Grape Playlot Park
N. Mozart St. & N. Avondale Ave.
(2832 W & 2850 N)

playground, 2 sandboxes.

Graver Park
1518 W. 102nd Pl.
238-6913

athletic field, 2 jr. baseball, softball, football & soccer, 4 tennis,
2 horseshoes, volleyball, 6 basketball stds., 2 playgrounds, 2 sandboxes, 2 ice-skating, day camp,
multiple-use paved area, fieldhouse, assembly hall, 5 clubrooms, craft shop, kitchen.

Green Briar Park
2650 W. Peterson Ave. (6000 N)
764-3008

2 jr. baseball, tennis, volleyball,
multiple-use paved area, 4 basketball stds., playground, spray pool,
sandbox, ice-skating, day camp,
fieldhouse, gymnasium, assembly
hall, 7 clubrooms, kitchen, artcraft, camera club, lapidary shop,
yoga, enameling.

Greenebaum Playlot Park
1701-55 N. Kildare Ave. (4300 W)

softball, multiple-use paved area, 4
basketball stds., volleyball, playground spray pool, sandbox, ice-
skating.

CITY CENTER PARKS

Gross Playground Park
2708 W. Lawrence Ave. (4800 N)
878-5614

softball, horseshoes, 2 multiple-use paved areas, 4 basketball stds., 2 volleyball, playground, spray pool, sandbox, 2 ice-skating, recreation building, clubroom.

Haas Playground Park
2402 N. Washtenaw (2700 W)
276-1332

softball, multiple-use paved area, 5 basketball stds., volleyball, playground, spray pool, sandbox, ice-skating, recreation building, 2 clubrooms.

Hale Park
6140 S. Melvina Ave. (6200 W)
586-3834 or 586-2920

swimming pool, athletic field, baseball, 3 softball, football & soccer, 2 tennis, multiple-use paved area, 4 volleyball, 4 basketball stds., playground, sandbox, ice-skating, day camp, gymnasium, assembly hall, 4 clubrooms, kitchen, artcraft, music, recreation building, clubroom.

Hamilton Park
513 W. 72nd St.
783-5657

swimming pool, athletic field,
4 baseball, 7 softball, football &
soccer, running track (6 lap), 8
tennis, 5 volleyball, 2 handball, 6
horseshoes, 6 basketball stds.,
multiple-use paved area, playground, spray pool, sandbox, ice-
skating, bicycle path, day camp,
fieldhouse, 2 gymnasiums, 2
assembly halls, 7 clubrooms, craft
shop, kitchen, public library,
archery range, yoga.

Hamlin Park
3035 N. Hoyne Ave. (2100 W)
472-3001
Craft Shop—935-7975

swimming pool, athletic field,
2 baseball, 2 jr. baseball, football
& soccer, 2 tennis, multiple-use
paved area, 4 basketball stds., 2
volleyball, playground, 2 ice-
skating, day camp, chess/
checker tables, fieldhouse, 2 gymnasiums, assembly hall, 4 clubrooms, craft shop, kitchen, drama,
senior citizen center, music.

Harding Playground Park
4912 S. Calumet Ave. (344 E)

multiple-use paved area, volleyball, 2 basketball stds., playground, ice-skating, recreation
building, clubroom.

Harding Playlot Park
3917-25 W. Division St. (1200 N)

multiple-use paved area, 2 basketball stds., playground.

Harper Playground Park
6407 S. Harper Ave. (1532 E)

softball, playground, sandbox,
recreation building (not in use).

Harrison Park
1824 S. Wood St. (1800 W)
294-4714

athletic field, 2 baseball, 2 jr.
baseball, 2 softball, 2 football &
soccer, 2 tennis, 6 horseshoes,
multiple-use paved area, 8 basketball stds., 4 volleyball, playground, spray pool, 2 sandboxes, 2
ice-skating, bicycle path, fieldhouse, natatorium, 2 gymnasiums,
combination assembly hall, 2 clubrooms, boat building shop,
kitchen, music, craft shop.

Hasan Playlot Park
6851-59 S. Oglesby Ave. (2332 E)

playground, sandbox.

Hawthorne Playlot Park
1200-22 W. 77th St.

4 basketball stds., playground,
spray pool, sandbox, multiple-
use paved area.

Hayes Park
2936 W. 85th St.
776-4441

athletic field, 2 baseball, 4 jr.
baseball, 2 football & soccer, 2
tennis, multiple-use paved area, 4
basketball stds., 4 volleyball, playground, spray pool, 2 ice-skating,

day camp, sandbox, fieldhouse, gymnasium, 3 clubrooms, kitchen, craft shop, yoga.

Hermitage Park
5839 W. Wood St. (1800 W)
925-0041

athletic field, softball, football & soccer, 2 horseshoes, multiple-use paved area, 2 basketball stds., playground, spray pool, sandbox, ice-skating, recreation building, clubroom.

Hermitage Playlot Park
4249 N. Hermitage Ave. (1732 W)

playground, spray pool, sandbox.

Hermosa Park
2240 N. Kilbourn Ave. (4500 W)
235-1638

athletic field, baseball, jr. baseball, 2 softball, football & soccer, 4 tennis, 4 horseshoes, multiple-use paved area, 4 shuffleboard, volleyball, 2 basketball stds., playground, spray pool, sandbox, ice-skating, day camp, fieldhouse, assembly hall, 5 clubrooms, kitchen, artcraft.

Hiawatha Park
8029 W. Forest Preserve Dr. (3500 N)
625-4770

athletic field, 3 baseball, football & soccer, 2 tennis, playground, 2 ice-skating, day camp, sandbox, field-

house, gymnasium, 7 clubrooms, artcraft, drama, craft shop, kitchen, recreation building, clubroom, drama, senior citizen center, yoga.

Hickory Playlot Park
4834 N. Winthrop Ave. (1100 W)

playground, sandbox.

Hoard Playground Park
E 72nd St. & S. Dobson Ave. (1032 E)

3 multiple-use paved areas, spray pool, jr. baseball, 8 basketball stds., playground.

Holly Playlot Park
4046-56 S. Ellis Ave. (1000 E)

playground, spray pool.

Hollywood Park
3312 W. Thorndale Ave. (5934 N)
267-7432

2 softball, tennis, horseshoes, multiple-use paved area, 4 basketball stds., 2 volleyball, playground, spray pool, 2 sandboxes, ice-skating, day camp, recreation building, 4 clubrooms, kitchen.

Holstein Park
2200 N. Oakley Ave. (2300 W)
276-3189

swimming pool, 2 softball, 2 basketball stds., playground, sandbox, 2 ice-skating, day camp, fieldhouse, 2 gymnasiums, assembly hall, 3 clubrooms, senior citizen center, yoga.

Homan Playlot Park
2146-50 S. Homan Ave. (3400 W)

playground, sandbox.

Honeysuckle Playlot Park
4635-39 S. Champlain Ave. (635 E)

playground, sandbox.

Horan Playground Park
3035 W. Van Buren St. (400 S)
826-7121

softball, 3 basketball stds., playground, spray pool, ice-skating, sandbox, recreation building, 2 clubrooms.

Hornbeam Playlot Park
1416-26 S. Hamlin Ave. (3800 W)

playground, sandbox, spray pool.

Horner Park
2741 W. Montrose Ave. (4400 N)
267-2444
Fieldhouse—267-0120

athletic field, 3 baseball, 3 jr. baseball, 6 softball, 4 football & soccer, 4 tennis, multiple-use paved area, 4 basketball stds., 4 volleyball, playground, ice-skating, day camp, bicycle path, fieldhouse, 2 gymnasiums, 5 clubrooms, craft shop, 2 kitchens, artcraft, drama, art center, music, yoga.

CITY CENTER PARKS

Hoyne Playground Park
3417 S. Hamilton Ave. (2132 W)
247-8731

jr. baseball, multiple-use paved area, volleyball, 6 basketball stds., playground, sandbox, 2 ice-skating, recreation building, clubroom.

Hubbard Playlot Park
4942-58 W. Hubbard St. (440 N)

multiple-use paved area, 2 basketball stds., playground, spray pool, sandbox.

Huckleberry Playlot Park
6200 S. Kimbark Ave. (1300 E)

playground, 4 basketball stds., volleyball.

Hudson Playground Park
421 W. Locust St. (900 N)
294-4726

4 basketball stds., playground, spray pool, sandbox, ice-skating, recreation building, clubroom.

Humboldt Park
W. North & N. Humboldt Aves. (1600 N & 3000 W)
Craft Shop—1400 N. Sacramento Ave.   276-3892

swimming lagoon, swimming pool, 2 athletic fields, 3 baseball, 6 jr. baseball, softball, 2 football & soccer, 12 tennis, 6 volleyball, 2 multiple-use paved areas, 8 basketball stds., 5 playgrounds, 2 spray pools, 3 sandboxes, 2 ice-skating, day camp, bicycle path, fishing lagoon, fieldhouse, 2 gymnasiums, combination assembly hall, 4 clubrooms, craft shop, kitchen, boat building shop.

Hyacinth Playlot Park
4534-40 S. Greenwood Ave. (1100 E)

3 multiple-use paved areas, 8 basketball stds., 2 volleyball, playground, spray pool.

Independence Park
3945 N. Springfield Ave. (3900 W)
578-1039

3 softball, 4 tennis, 5 horseshoes, 2 basketball stds., playground, spray pool, 2 sandboxes, 2 ice-skating, day camp, special recreation program, fieldhouse, natatorium, gymnasium, assembly hall, 4 clubrooms, craft shop, 2 kitchens, artcraft, senior citizen center, camera club.

Indian Boundary Park
2500 W. Lunt Ave. (7000 N)
764-7678
Zoo—2555 W. Estes Ave.
274-0200

4 tennis, volleyball, 2 basketball stds., volleyball, 2 horseshoes, playground, spray pool, sandbox,

2 ice-skating, day camp, recreation building, clubroom, kitchen.

Indiana & 56th Playlot Park
5635 S. Indiana Ave. (200 E)

multiple-use paved area, playground.

Ivy Playlot Park
1642 W. 35th St.

4 basketball stds.

Jackson (Natatorium) Park
3506 W. Fillmore (1024 S)
638-1310

natatorium building.

Jackson Playlot Park
4319 S. Indiana Ave. (200 E)

playground, spray pool, sandbox.

Jacob Park
4674-4708 N. Virginia Ave. (2750 W)

playground, sandbox.

Jefferson Park
4822 N. Long Ave. (5400 W)
545-3992
Craft Shop—685-4281

athletic field, baseball, 2 softball, football & soccer, 4 tennis, volleyball, 4 basketball stds., playground, spray pool, sandbox, ice-skating, day camp, fieldhouse, gymnasium, assembly hall, 8 clubrooms, kitchen, music, artcraft, lapidary shop, senior citizen center.

55

CITY CENTER PARKS

Jefferson Playlot Park
1640 S. Jefferson St. (600 W)

jr. baseball, multiple-use paved area, 2 basketball stds., playground, spray pool, sandbox, ice-skating.

Jensen Playground Park
4600 N. Lawndale Ave. (3700 W)
463-1026

jr. baseball, tennis, 4 basketball stds., 2 multiple-use paved areas, 5 volleyball, playground, spray pool, sandbox, 2 ice-skating, day camp, recreation building, 2 clubrooms, kitchen.

Jonquil Playlot Park
1025-47 W. Wrightwood Ave. (2600 N)

jr. baseball, playground, ice-skating, 3 horseshoes, chess/checker tables.

Juniper Playlot Park
3652-58 N. Greenview Ave. (1500 W)

playground, spray pool, chess/checker tables.

Kedvale Playground Park
4134 W. Hirsch St. (1400 N)
235-5984

volleyball, 2 basketball stds., playground, ice-skating, spray pool, recreation building, 2 clubrooms.

Keeler Playlot Park
1243 S. Keeler Ave. (4200 W)

playground.

Kells Playground Park
3201 W. Chicago AVe. (800 N)

jr. baseball, playground, ice-skating, basketball std., toilet building.

Kelly Park
4136 S. California Ave. (2800 W)
927-1663, 927-1664

athletic field, 2 baseball, 2 jr. baseball, football & soccer, 2 multiple-use paved areas, 6 basketball stds., 2 volleyball, playground, 2 ice-skating, day camp (& play camp), natatorium, 2 gymnasiums, assembly hall, 4 clubrooms, kitchen, music, recreation building, clubroom, drama.

Kelvyn Park
4438 W. Wrightwood Ave. (2600 N)
252-8547

athletic field, 2 jr. baseball, football & soccer, 4 tennis, 7 horseshoes, multiple-use paved area, 2 basketball stds., 2 volleyball, 4 shuffleboard, playground, spray pool, sandbox, ice-skating, day camp, bicycle path, fieldhouse, gymnasium, assembly hall, 5 clubrooms, craft shop, kitchen, senior citizen center.

Kenmore Playlot Park
3141 N. Kenmore Ave. (1040 W)

multiple-use paved area, basketball std., playground.

Kennedy Park
11320 S. Western Ave. (2400 W)
445-8657

swimming pool, athletic field, baseball, 4 jr. baseball, softball, 2 football & soccer, 4 tennis, 2 horseshoes, 2 volleyball, 6 basketball stds., playground, sandbox, ice-skating, day camp, fieldhouse, 5 clubrooms, music, kitchen, senior citizen center.

Kensington Playground Park
11800 S. Calumet Ave. (344 E)
785-4363

athletic field, baseball, 3 softball, football & soccer, multiple-use paved area, 2 basketball stds., playground, spray pool, sandbox, ice-skating, day camp, recreation building, clubroom.

Ken-We Playground Park
2945 N. Kenosha Ave. (4238 W)
725-5731

athletic field, softball, jr. baseball, 2 volleyball, multiple-use paved area, 2 basketball stds., play-

ground, sandbox, ice-skating, spray pool, day camp, football & soccer, recreation building, clubroom.

Kenwood Park
1330 E. 50th St.
268-4432, 924-9373

athletic field, 3 jr. baseball, football & soccer, 2 tennis, multiple-use paved area, 4 basketball stds., 4 volleyball, playground, spray pool, sandbox, ice-skating, day camp, gymnasium, combination assembly hall, 6 clubrooms, kitchen, artcraft, drama, recreation building, clubroom, music.

Keystone Playlot Park
1653-57 N. Keystone Ave. (4032 W)

playground, sandbox.

Kilbourn Park
3501 N. Kilbourn Ave. (4500 W)
725-1597

athletic field, baseball, jr. baseball, softball, football & soccer, running track (4 lap), 8 tennis, 2 volleyball, 6 horseshoes, 5 basketball stds., playground, spray pool, sandbox, 2 ice-skating, day camp, multiple-use paved area, fieldhouse, assembly hall, 8 clubrooms, craft shop, kitchen.

Kiwanis Playground Park
3315 W. Carmen AVe. (5100 N)
761-0038

softball, multiple-use paved area, basketball std., volleyball, playground, spray pool, sandbox, 2 ice-skating, recreation building, clubroom.

Kiwanis Playground Park
7631 N. Ashland Ave. (1600 W)
761-0038

softball, multiple-use paved area, basketball std., volleyball, playground, spray pool, sandbox, 2 ice-skating, recreation building, clubroom.

Kolmar Playlot Park
W. Berteau & N. Kolmar Aves. (4200 N & 4550 W)

jr. baseball, playground, ice-skating, sandbox.

Korczak Playlot Park
6152-58 N. Claremont (2332 W)

playground, sandbox.

Kosciuszko Park
2732 N. Avers Ave. (3832 W)
252-2596

athletic field, 4 softball, football & soccer, 3 tennis, multiple-use paved area, 2 basketball stds., volleyball, ice-skating, day camp, natatorium, fieldhouse, 2 gymnasiums, combination assembly

hall, 7 clubrooms, kitchen, drama, artcraft, senior citizen center, yoga.

LaFollette Park
1333 N. Laramie Ave. (5200 W)
378-0124

athletic field, jr. baseball, 4 softball, football & soccer, running track (4 lap), 6 tennis, multiple-use paved area, 2 volleyball, 4 shuffleboard, 2 basketball stds., 2 playgrounds, spray pool, 2 sandboxes, 2 ice-skating, day camp, bicycle path, 6 horseshoes, fieldhouse, 2 gymnasiums, combination assembly hall, 7 clubrooms, kitchen, drama, artcraft, senior citizen center, yoga.

Lake Meadows Park
3113 S. Rhodes Ave. (500 E)
294-4697

athletic field, 2 jr. baseball, football & soccer, multiple-use paved area, 4 basketball stds., playground, day camp, 2 volleyball, shuffleboard, gymnasium, combination assembly hall, 4 clubrooms, artcraft, music, yoga.

Lake Park Ave. Playlot Park
3756 S. Lake Park Ave. (900 E)

basketball std., playground, sandbox.

Langley Playlot Park
E. 113th St. & S. Langley Ave. (700 E)

basketball std., playground, sandbox.

Lavergne Playlot Park
W. Lawrence & N. Lavergne Aves. (4800 N & 5000 W)

playground.

59

Lawler Park
5210 W. 64th St.
735-8130

athletic field, 2 softball, football & soccer, 2 horseshoes, 2 multiple-use paved areas, 6 basketball stds., playground, spray pool, sandbox, ice-skating, day camp, volleyball, recreation building, clubroom, kitchen, artcraft.

Le Claire-Hearst Community Park
5116 W. 44th St.
581-3084

2 jr. baseball, 2 tennis, 4 basketball stds., playground, swimming pool (on CHA Le Claire Courts property), multiple-use paved area, day camp, fieldhouse, gymnasium, 5 clubrooms, kitchen, music, artcraft, craft shop.

Lee Playlot Park
W. 87th St. & S. Lawndale Ave. (3700 W)

playground, sandbox.

Legion Park
W. Peterson Ave. to W. Foster Ave. & North Shore Branch of Chicago River (5600 N & 3032 W)

2 jr. baseball, 12 horseshoes, 2 multiple-use paved areas, 8 basketball stds., 2 volleyball, 6 playgrounds, 5 sandboxes, bicycle path, 2 tennis.

Leone Park & Beach
1222 W. Touhy Ave. (7200 N)

sandbox, bathing beach, 2 ice-skating, day camp, playground, fieldhouse.

Lerner Park
7000 N. Sacramento Ave. (3000 W)

2 jr. baseball, 2 tennis, multiple-use paved area, 4 basketball stds., 4 volleyball, playground, sandbox.

Levin Park
N. Pine Ave. & W. Ferdinand St. (5500 W & 462 N)

jr. baseball, volleyball, playground, ice-skating, 4 basketball stds., sandbox.

Lily Gardens Park
S. Lowe Ave. (632 W) to C.&W.I. R.R. & W. 71st St. to W. 73rd St.

passive recreation area, 2 lagoons.

Lindblom Park
5930 S. Damen Ave. (2000 W)
776-8788

athletic field, 2 baseball, jr. baseball, 3 softball, football & soccer, 2 tennis, 6 volleyball, 2 horseshoes, multiple-use paved area, 6 basketball stds., playground, ice-skating, recreation building, clubroom.

Linden Playlot Park
1129-47 N. Pulaski Rd. (4000 W)

4 basketball stds., playground, spray pool, sandbox.

Locust Playlot Park
7105 S. Wentworth Ave. (200 W)

4 basketball stds., playground.

London Playlot Park
W. 18th St. & S. Trumbull Ave. (3432 W)

playground.

Longwood Playground Park
W. 91st St. & S. Longwood Dr. (2100 W)

3 tennis, playground, 2 ice-skating.

Lowe Playground Park
5203 S. Lowe Ave. (632 W)
285-6388

athletic field, baseball, 2 jr. baseball, football & soccer, horseshoes, volleyball, multiple-use paved area, 2 basketball stds., playground, spray pool, sandbox, 2 ice-skating, day camp, recreation building, clubroom.

Loyola Park
1230 W. Greenleaf Ave. (7032 N)
262-0690

athletic field, baseball, 2 softball, football & soccer, 4 tennis, 2 handball, 3 shuffleboard, multiple-use paved area, 2 volleyball, playground, bathing beach, day camp, ice-skating, fieldhouse, 2 gymnasiums, combination assembly hall, 6 clubrooms, craft shop, 2 kitchens, artcraft, drama, art center, senior citizen center, yoga.

CITY CENTER PARKS

Luella Playlot Park
E. 100th St. & S. Luella Ave.
(2232 E)

multiple-use paved area, 2 basketball stds., volleyball, playground, sandbox.

Lunt Playlot Park
2237-39 W. Lunt Ave. (7000 N)

playground, spray pool, sandbox.

Lyle Park
W. 76th St. to W. 79th St.
& S. Wallace St. (600 W)

passive recreation area, playground, sandbox.

Madden Park
3800 S. Rhodes Ave. (532 E)
285-1444

swimming pool, athletic field, 2 jr. baseball, 2 softball, football & soccer, running track (6 lap), multiple-use paved area, volleyball, 2 horseshoes, 2 basketball stds., playground, spray pool, 2 sandboxes, ice-skating, day camp, gymnasium, 5 clubrooms, kitchen, music, senior citizen center, artcraft, art center.

Magnolia Playlot Park
3223-30 W. Flournoy St. (700 S)

playground, spray pool.

Malus Playlot Park
5416-36 S. Shields Ave. (332 W)

playground, sandbox.

Mann Park
E. 130th St. & S. Carondolet Ave.
(3035 E)
646-2633

athletic field, baseball, 3 jr. baseball, 2 softball, football & soccer, 4 tennis, multiple-use paved area, 5 volleyball, 4 basketball stds., playground, spray pool, sandbox, 2 ice-skating, day camp, fieldhouse, natatorium, 2 gymnasiums, combination assembly hall, 4 clubrooms, craft shop, kitchen, artcraft, drama.

Maple Playlot Park
2047 N. Spaulding Ave. (3300 W)

multiple-use paved area, playground, sandbox.

Maplewood Playground Park
1640 N. Maplewood Ave. (2532 W)
384-7166

softball, multiple-use paved area, 4 basketball stds., volleyball, horseshoes, playground, spray pool, sandbox, ice-skating, recreation building, clubroom.

Marigold Playlot Park
3101-19 W. Fulton Blvd. (300 N)

multiple-use paved area, 4 basketball stds., playground.

Marquette Park
6734 S. Kedzie Ave.
776-9879

Marshfield Playground Park
1637 W. 87th St.
445-9456

softball, basketball stds., playground, spray pool, ice-skating,
recreation building, clubroom.

Mather Park
5835 N. Lincoln Ave. (2800 W)
561-1460, 271-2996

athletic field, baseball, 4 jr. baseball, 2 football & soccer, 6 tennis,
4 horseshoes, multiple-use paved
area, 4 basketball stds., 4 volleyball, playground, sandbox, 2 ice-
skating, day camp, natatorium, 2
gymnasiums, assembly hall, 5
clubrooms, recreation building,
clubroom, kitchen.

Mayfair Park
4550 W. Sunnyside Ave. (4500 N)
545-4049

athletic field, 2 jr. baseball, football & soccer, 2 basketball stds.,
multiple-use paved area, 2 volleyball, 2 shuffleboard, playground,
spray pool, sandbox, ice-skating,
day camp, fieldhouse, assembly
hall, 4 clubrooms, kitchen, artcraft.

CITY CENTER PARKS

McGuane Park
2901 S. Poplar Ave. (1000 W)
294-4692

athletic field, baseball, 2 jr. baseball, softball, football & soccer, multiple-use paved area, 4 basketball stds., volleyball, 4 shuffleboard, playground, ice-skating, day camp, spray pool, fieldhouse, natatorium, gymnasium, 6 clubrooms, craft shop, kitchen, senior citizen center.

McInerney Playlot Park
4446-58 S. Emerald Ave. (731 W)

McKeon Playlot Park
W. 36th St. & S. Wallace St. (600 W)

multiple-use paved area, play-ground, sandbox.

McKiernan Playground Park
10714 S. Sawyer Ave. (3232 W)
445-2921

athletic field, 2 jr. baseball, football & soccer, multiple-use paved area, 2 basketball stds., volleyball, playground, sandbox, ice-skating, day camp, spray pool, recreation building, 2 clubrooms, music.

McKinley Park
2210 W. Pershing Rd. (3900 S)
523-3811

swimming pool, 2 athletic fields, 3 baseball, jr. baseball, 6 softball, football & soccer, 14 tennis, 2 handball, volleyball, 2 multiple-use paved areas, 8 basketball stds., playground, spray pool, 2 ice-skating, day camp, bicycle path, casting pool, fishing lagoon, sand-box, fieldhouse, 2 gymnasiums, assembly hall, 2 clubrooms, kitchen, art craft, music, senior citizen center.

McLaren Playlot Park
1520 W. Polk St. (800 S)

playground, sandbox.

Mellin Park
W. Bryn Mawr & N. Ashland Aves. (5600 N & 1600 W)

passive recreation area, play-ground, sandbox.

Memorial Playground Park
149 W. 73rd St.
483-2762

athletic field, jr. baseball, softball, football & soccer, multiple-use paved area, 3 basketball stds., 2 volleyball, playground, sandbox, ice-skating, day camp, recreation building, clubroom.

Merrill Playground Park
E. 96th St. to E. 97th St. & S. Merrill Ave. (2132 E)

jr. baseball, multiple-use paved

area, 4 basketball stds., volleyball, playground, sandbox, spray pool.

Merrimac Park
6343 W. Irving Park Rd. (4000 N)
725-5080

athletic field, jr. baseball, 2 softball, football & soccer, 2 tennis, volleyball, 2 horseshoes, 6 basketball stds., playground, spray pool, sandbox, 2 ice-skating, day camp, multiple-use paved area, fieldhouse, gymnasium, craft shop, 5 clubrooms, kitchen, artcraft, senior citizen center.

Merryman Playlot Park
3736 N. Marshfield Ave. (1632 W)

playground, sandbox.

Meyering Playground Park
7140 S. King Dr. (400 E)
723-3150

swimming pool, athletic field, 2 jr. baseball, softball, football & soccer, multiple-use paved area, 2 basketball stds., volleyball, playground, play slab, sandbox, iceskating, day camp, recreation building, 2 clubrooms.

Micek Playground Park
5311 S. Hamilton Ave. (2132 W)
778-4520

softball, multiple-use paved area, 2 basketball stds., playground, iceskating, spray pool, day camp, recreation building, clubroom.

65

Midway Plaisance Park
W. 59th St. to W. 60th St. & S. Stony Island to S. Cottage Grove Ave.

passive recreation area, 2 ice-skating, bicycle path, bridle path.

Millard Playlot Park
1329-31 S. Millard Ave. (3632 W)

multiple-use paved area, 2 basketball stds., playground, sandbox.

Miller Playlot Park
846-48 S. Miller St. (1029 W)

playground, sandbox.

Minuteman Park
W. 59th St. & S. Central Ave. (5600 W)
582-1818

baseball, 2 jr. baseball, 2 multiple-use paved areas, 8 basketball stds., 2 tennis, 2 playgrounds, 2 sandboxes, day camp.

Mock Orange Playlot Park
1746-52 W. Juneway Ter. (7736 N)

playground.

Montgomery Playlot Park
W. 66th St. & S. Talman Ave. (2632 W)

playground, sandbox.

Monticello Playlot Park
1810-18 N. Monticello Ave. (3632 W)

multiple-use paved area, 2 basketball stds., playground.

Monument Park
N. Avondale & N. Oliphant Aves. (6700 N & 7625 W)

passive recreation area, playground.

Moore Playground Park
5085 W. Adams St. (200 S)
287-8384

2 jr. baseball, multiple-use paved area, 2 basketball stds., volleyball, playground, spray pool, sandbox, ice-skating, day camp, recreation building, 2 clubrooms.

Moran Playground Park
5727 S. Racine Ave. (1200 W)
436-0141

2 basketball stds., playground, spray pool, sandbox, ice-skating, day camp, recreation building, 2 clubrooms.

Morgan Field Park
11710 S. Morgan St. (1000 W)
568-6969

multiple-use paved area, 4 basketball stds., 2 volleyball, playground, sandbox, ice-skating, day camp, gymnasium, combination assembly hall, 5 clubrooms, drama.

Morse Playlot Park
6925-49 N. Ridge Blvd. (2100 W)

playground, sandbox.

Mt. Greenwood Park
3721 W. 111th St.
779-0650
Craft Shop—239-2599

swimming pool, athletic field, 2 baseball, 6 softball, football & soccer, 4 tennis, multiple-use paved area, 4 basketball stds., 5 volleyball, playground, spray pool, sandbox, 2 ice-skating, bicycle path, day camp, special recreation program, field house, gymnasium, 7 clubrooms, craft shop, kitchen, art center, recreation building, 2 clubrooms, kitchen, artcraft, music ceramics, senior citizens center, yoga.

MT. Vernon Park
10540 S. Morgan St. (1000 W)
779-3497

athletic field, baseball, 4 jr. baseball, football & soccer, 2 multiple-use paved areas, 4 basketball stds., 3 volleyball, playground, sandbox, 2 ice-skating, gymnasium, assembly hall, 4 clubrooms, kitchen, artcraft, music, recreation building, clubroom.

Mozart Park
2036 N. Avers Ave. (3832 W)
227-1469

athletic field, jr. baseball, softball, football & soccer, 3 horseshoes, multiple-use paved area, 2 basketball stds., volleyball, 4 shuffleboard, playground, spray pool, ice-skating, fieldhouse, 3 clubrooms, kitchen, senior citizen center.

Mulberry Playlot
3150 Robinson Court 1632 W)

playground, spray pool, sandbox.

CITY CENTER PARKS

Munroe Park
2617 W. 105th St.
445-7284

athletic field, 2 jr. baseball, football & soccer, 2 tennis, multiple-use paved area, volleyball, playground, spray pool, sandbox, ice-skating, day camp, recreation building, clubroom.

Murray Playground Park
1743 W. 73rd St.
476-0898

athletic field, baseball, 2 softball, 2 multiple-use paved areas, 4 basketball stds., volleyball, playground, sandbox, ice-skating, recreation building, 2 clubrooms.

Nelson Playlot Park
2951-53 W. Nelson St. (3032 N)

playground, spray pool, sandbox.

Ninebark Playlot Park
1447-53 S. Harding Ave. (3932 W)

playground, spray pool.

Normandy Playground Park
6660 W. 52nd St.
586-0210

athletic field, 2 softball, football & soccer, 2 multiple-use paved areas, 2 basketball stds., volleyball, playground, spray pool, ice-skating, day camp, recreation building, clubroom, artcraft.

North Mayfair Playlot Park
4533-39 W. Carmen Ave. (5100 N)

playground, sandbox.

Norwood Park
5801 N. Natoma Ave. (6632 W)
631-3994
Craft Shop—631-7608

swimming pool, 2 athletic fields, baseball, 2 jr. baseball, football & soccer, running track (6 lap), 6 tennis, 2 horseshoes, multiple-use paved area, 4 basketball stds., 2 volleyball, 4 shuffleboard, playground, ice-skating, day camp, fieldhouse, gymnasium, combination assembly hall, 2 clubrooms, craft shop, kitchen, artcraft, art center, senior citizen center.

Norwood Playground Park
6801 W. Imlay St. (6450 N)

4 basketball stds., playground, sandbox, spray pool.

Oak Playlot Park
2133 N. McVicker Ave. (6032 W)

multiple-use paved area, 2 basketball stds., playground, sandbox.

Oakdale Park
965 W. 95th St.
445-9888

swimming pool, athletic field, baseball, 3 softball, football & soccer, multiple-use paved area,

4 basketball stds., playground, spray pool, sandbox, ice-skating, day camp, volleyball, recreation building, 2 clubrooms, kitchen, artcraft.

Oakdale Playlot Park
901-99 W. Oakdale Ave. (2932 N)

playground, spray pool, sandbox.

Oakenwald Playlot Park
4570 S. Oakenwald Ave. (1000 E)

playground, sandbox.

Oakland Playlot Park
S. Lake Park Ave. (900 E)
& E. 39th St. I.C.R.R.

playground, sandbox.

Oakley Playground Park
2251 W. 50th Pl.
925-0720

softball, horseshoes, volleyball, basketball std., playground, sandbox, ice-skating, spray pool, day camp, recreation building, clubroom.

Oakley Playlot Park
6441 S. Oakley Ave. (2300 W)

playground spray pool, sandbox.

Ogden Park
6500 S. Racine Ave. (1220 W)
873-1038

swimming pool, athletic field, baseball, 3 jr. baseball, 6 softball, 2 football & soccer, running track (4 lap), 4 tennis, 6 horseshoes, 5 volleyball, 2 multiple-use paved areas, 8 basketball stds., 3 playgrounds, spray pool, sandbox, ice-skating, day camp, bicycle path, fieldhouse, gymnasium, 6 clubrooms, artcraft, drama, art center.

O'Hallaren Park
8335 S Honore St. (1826 W)
445-5831

athletic field, 5 softball, football & soccer, 2 volleyball, 2 multiple-use paved areas, 4 basketball stds., playground, 2 sandboxes, 2 ice-skating, recreation building, clubroom.

Ohio & Harding Playlot Park
601-13 N. Harding Ave. (3932 W)

multiple-use paved area, 2 basketball stds., playground, sandbox.

Ohio Playlot Park
4712 W. Ohio St. (600 N)

multiple-use paved area, 2 basketball stds., playground, spray pool, sandbox.

Olympia Park
6566 N. Avondale Ave. (7530 W)
763-3787

athletic field, baseball, 2 jr. baseball, 2 softball, football &

soccer, 3 tennis, volleyball, 6 basketball stds., playground, spray pool, 3 sandboxes, 2 ice-skating, day camp, multiple-use paved area, fieldhouse, gymnasium, 6 clubrooms, kitchen, craft shop, artcraft, yoga.

Oriole Park
5430 N. Olcott Ave. (7500 W)
763-6069

2 athletic fields, 2 baseball, 4 jr. baseball, softball, 2 football & soccer, straightaway track (1 lap), 3 tennis, 2 multiple-use paved areas, 6 basketball stds., 3 volleyball, 2 playgrounds, sandbox, 2 ice-skating, day camp, bicycle path, fieldhouse, gymnasium, combination assembly hall, 4 clubrooms, kitchen, artcraft, senior citizen center, yoga.

Oz Park
601-733 W. Webster Ave. (2200 N)

athletic field, baseball, jr. baseball, football & soccer, 4 tennis, 2 horseshoes, shuffleboard, multiple-use paved area, 4 basketball stds., playground, volleyball, chess/checker tables.

Palmer Park
E. 111th St. & S. Indiana Ave. (200 E)

swimming pool, athletic field, 2 baseball, 10 softball, 3 football &

soccer, running track (6 lap), 12 tennis, 4 handball, multiple-use paved area, 2 volleyball, 3 shuffleboard, 2 playgrounds, 2 spray pools, sandbox, 2 ice-skating, day camp, bicycle path, wading pool, model yacht basin, 4 basketball stds., fieldhouse, 2 gymnasiums, assembly hall, 6 clubrooms, kitchen, artcraft.

Parkview Playground Park
3823 W. School St. (3300 N)
267-3345

softball, volleyball, playground, ice-skating, multiple-use paved area, 5 basketball stds., recreation building, clubroom.

Paschen Playground Park
1932 W. Lunt Ave. (7000 N)
274-2840

multiple-use paved area, 4 basketball stds., volleyball, playground, ice-skating, sandbox, 2 horseshoes, recreation building, 2 clubrooms.

Pasteur Park
4334 W. 58th St.
735-4654
Pasteur School Park
5825 S. Kostner Ave.
585-1466

athletic field, baseball, 2 jr. baseball, 2 softball, football & soccer, 2 tennis, multiple-use paved area, 4 basketball stds., 4 volleyball, playground, spray pool, 2 ice-skating, day camp, sandbox, gymnasium, assembly hall, 2 clubrooms, music, recreation building, clubroom.

People's Playlot Park
2550-58 W. Moffat St. (1850 N)

playground.

Periwinkle Playlot Park
W. 66th St. & S. Perry Ave. (100 W)

playground, spray pool.

Pietrowski Playground Park
9650 S. Avenue M (3532 E)
721-7386

3 basketball stds., playground, ice-skating, multiple-use paved area, recreation building, clubroom.

Pine Playlot Park
9501-13 S. Oglesby Ave. (2334 E)

playground, sandbox.

Piotrowski Park
W. 31st St. & S. Keeler Ave. (4200 (4200 W)
247-6131

athletic field, 2 baseball, 4 jr. baseball, 2 softball, football & soccer, 5 tennis, 2 la bocci, multiple-use paved area, 4 basketball stds., 4 volleyball, playground, spray

pool, sandbox, 2 ice-skating, day camp, bicycle path, fieldhouse, gymnasium, combination assembly hall, 7 clubrooms, craft shop, senior citizen center, music.

Plum Playlot Park
1122-44 W. Winona Ave. (5135 N)

playground, sandbox.

Poplar Playlot Park
4044-48 S. Prairie Ave. (300 E)

playground, spray pool.

Portage Park
4100 N. Long Ave. (5400 W)
545-4337
Gym Building
4101 N. Central Ave.
777-3660

swimming pool, athletic field, 2 baseball, jr. baseball, 2 softball, football & soccer, 9 tennis, volleyball, 8 horseshoes, 4 basketball stds., playground, spray pool, 2 sandboxes, 2 ice-skating, day camp, bicycle path, fieldhouse, natatorium, gymnasium, 2 clubrooms, craft shop, kitchen, artcraft, ceramics, senior citizen center, drama, camera club.

Pottawattomie Park
7340 N. Rogers Ave. (1900 W)
743-4313

athletic field, baseball, 2 jr. baseball, football & soccer, 2

tennis, 4 basketball stds., playground, spray pool, sandbox, 2 ice-skating, day camp, multiple-use paved area, special recreation program, fieldhouse, gymnasium, combination assembly hall, 4 clubrooms, kitchen, artcraft, 2 handball, drama, yoga.

Privet Playlot Park
1844 N. Sheffield Ave. (1000 W)

playground.

Pulaski Park
1419 W. Blackhawk St. (1500 N)
294-4705

swimming pool, 2 jr. baseball, volleyball, multiple-use paved area, 2 basketball stds., playground, spray pool, sandbox, ice-skating, day camp, fieldhouse, 2 gymnasiums, assembly hall, 6 clubrooms, craft shop, kitchen, artcraft, senior citizen center, archery range.

Pulaski Playlot Park
5642 N. Pulaski Rd. (4000 W)

playground, sandbox.

Quayle Playlot Park
4001-11 S. Lake Park Ave. (940 E)

playground, multiple-use paved area, 4 basketball stds., chess/checker tables.

Racine-Draper Playlot Park
2522-34 N. Racine Ave. (1200 W)

multiple-use paved area, 2 basketball stds., playground, sandbox.

CITY CENTER PARKS

Rainey Park
4350 W. 79th St.
582-1424

athletic field, 2 baseball, 2 jr. baseball, football & soccer, 3 tennis, multiple-use paved area, 4 basketball stds., 4 volleyball, playground, sandbox, 2 ice-skating, day camp, gymnasium, combination assembly hall, 4 clubrooms, music.

Redbud Playlot Park
8213-17 S. Euclid Ave. (1932 E)

playground.

Revere Park
2509 W. Irving Park Rd. (4000 N)
539-4694

athletic field, baseball, 2 jr. baseball, softball, 3 football & soccer, 2 tennis, multiple-use paved area, 6 basketball stds., playground, spray pool, 2 sandboxes, ice-skating, day camp, fieldhouse, gymnasium, assembly hall, 5 clubrooms, kitchen, artcraft, drama, Revere Boys' Club Building, 8 clubrooms, senior citizen center, art center.

Ridge Park
9625 S. Longwood Dr. (1836 W)
238-1655
Pottery Studio—778-1138

athletic field, 2 jr. baseball, softball, football & soccer, 2 tennis, volleyball, playground, sandbox, 2 ice-skating, day camp, fieldhouse, natatorium, gymnasium, assembly hall, 9 clubrooms, craft shop, kitchen, artcraft, drama, enameling, art gallery, camera club, lapidary shop, ceramics, music, yoga.

Riis Park
6100 W. Fullerton Ave. (2400 N)
637-8952

swimming pool, 2 athletic fields, 2 baseball, 3 jr. baseball, 4 softball, football & soccer, running track (4 lap), 10 tennis, 6 horseshoes, 3 volleyball, 3 multiple-use paved areas, 6 basketball stds., 4 shuffleboard, 2 playgrounds, spray pool, 2 sandboxes, 2 ice-skating, day camp, bicycle path, archery range, lagoon, casting pool — pier, 2 la bocci, fieldhouse, gymnasium, assembly hall, 4 clubrooms, kitchen, artcraft, drama, archery range, craft shop.

River Park
5100 N. Francisco Ave. (2900 W)
561-2145

swimming pool, 2 athletic fields, 2 baseball, 5 jr. baseball, 2 football & soccer, 7 tennis, volleyball, 5 horseshoes, 6 basketball stds., 2 playgrounds, 2 spray pools, 4 sandboxes, 2 ice-skating, day camp, archery range, bicycle path, fieldhouse, gymnasium, assembly hall, 11 clubrooms, craft shop, kitchen, drama, camera club, senior citizen center, yoga.

Roberts Square Playground Park
5200-58 W. Argyle St. (5000 N)

playground, sandbox.

Robichaux Park
W. 93rd St. &
S. Eggleston Ave. (432 W)
488-3632

athletic field, 3 jr. baseball, 2 multiple-use paved areas, 2 tennis, 8 basketball stds., playground,

spray pool, sandbox, day camp, fieldhouse, gymnasium, combination assembly hall, 4 clubrooms, kitchen, drama, yoga.

Rogers Park
7345 N. Washtenaw Ave. (2700 W)
262-4772

athletic field, 2 baseball, 4 softball, football & soccer, 4 tennis, 8 basketball stds., playground, 2 ice-skating, day camp, bicycle path, sandbox, gymnasium, assembly hall, 4 clubrooms, kitchen.

CITY CENTER PARKS

Ronan Park
W. Argyle St. to W. Ainslie St.
& North Shore Branch of Chicago
River (5000 N & 3000 W)

playground, sandbox.

Roosevelt Playlot Park
2160 W. Roosevelt Rd. (1200 S)

playground.

Roscoe Playlot Park
667-69 W. Roscoe St. (3400 N)

playground, sandbox.

Rose Playlot Park
821-33 W. 19th St.

4 basketball stds.

Rosedale Park
6312 W. Rosedale Ave. (5832 N)

athletic field, 2 softball, football
& soccer, 2 tennis, volleyball, 6
basketball stds., 2 playgrounds,
spray pool, sandbox, 2 ice-
skating, day camp, fieldhouse,
gymnasium, combination
assembly hall, 6 clubrooms, 2
kitchens, artcraft, art center.

Rosenblum Park
7627 S. Constance Ave. (1836 E)
375-3468

athletic field, baseball, jr. baseball, 3 softball, football & soccer,
7 shuffleboard, multiple-use paved
area, 4 basketball stds., 4 volleyball, playground, sandbox, ice-
skating, day camp, natatorium,
2 gymnasiums, assembly hall,
4 clubrooms, kitchen, recreation
building, clubroom.

Rostenkowski Playlot Park
N. Greenview Ave. &
W. LeMoyne Ave.
(1500 W. & 1500 N)

softball, playground, spray pool.

Rowan Park
3535 E. 114th St.
646-4919

athletic field, 2 baseball, jr.
baseball, 2 softball, football &
soccer, straightway track (1 lap),
multiple-use paved area, 2 basketball stds., 2 volleyball, playground, sandbox, ice-skating, day
camp, 3 tennis, 2 gymnasiums,
assembly hall, 7 clubrooms,
kitchen, craft shop.

Russell Square Park
3045 E. 83rd St.
786-1434

swimming pool, athletic field,
baseball, 3 jr. baseball, football &
soccer, 6 tennis multiple-use
paved area, 4 basketball stds.,
volleyball, playground, spray pool,
sandbox, 2 ice-skating, day camp,
fieldhouse, gymnasium, 7 clubrooms, kitchen, artcraft, senior
citizen center.

Rutherford Sayre Park
6845 W. Belden Ave. (2300 N)
637-4035

athletic field, 2 jr. baseball, 2 softball, football & soccer, 3 tennis,
multiple-use paved area, 2 volleyball, 3 horseshoes, 6 basketball
stds., playground, spray pool,
sandbox, day camp, fieldhouse,
gymnasium, 4 clubrooms, kitchen,
artcraft, drama, yoga.

Sacramento Playlot Park
3520 N. Sacramento Ave. (3000 W)

softball, multiple-use paved area, 3
2 basketball stds., playground,
sandbox, ice-skating.

Sain Playground Park
2453 W. Monroe St. (100 S)

swimming pool, softball, playground, spray pool, sandbox,
recreation building, clubroom.

St. Louis Playlot Park
339-53 N. St. Louis Ave. (3500 W)

multiple-use paved area, 2 basketball stds., playground, spray pool.

Sauganash Park
5861 N. Kostner Ave. (4400 W)
545-9113

athletic field, 2 softball, football &
soccer, 2 tennis, volleyball, 2
horseshoes, 2 basketball stds.,
playground, sandbox, 2 ice-
skating, day camp, fieldhouse,

gymnasium, assembly hall, 5 club-rooms, kitchen, drama, artcraft, yoga.

Sayre Park
2311-13 N. Sayre Ave. (7000 W)

passive recreation area, 2 ice-skating.

Schaefer Playground Park
1552 W. Schreiber Ave. (6432 N)
743-2144

multiple-use paved area, volley-ball, 4 basketball stds., 2 shuffle-board, playground, sandbox, ice-skating, recreation building, clubroom, senior citizen center.

Scottsdale Playground Park
4637 W. 83rd St.
767-8442

athletic field, softball, jr. baseball, football & soccer, multiple-use paved area, 2 basketball stds., volleyball, playground, sandbox, ice-skating, recreation building, clubroom, kitchen.

Seneca Playlot Park
220-34 E. Chicago Ave. (800 N)

passive recreation area, play-ground, 2 sandboxes.

Senn Park
5900 N. Glenwood Ave. (1400 W)
784-4455

softball, 2 multiple-use paved areas, 8 basketball stds., 2 volley-ball, playground, sandbox, spray pool, day camp, ice-skating, natatorium, 2 gymnasiums, assembly hall, 4 clubrooms.

Seward Park
375 W. Elm St. (1138 N)
294-4727

athletic field, baseball, jr. baseball, softball, football & soccer,
multiple-use paved area, 2 volleyball, 4 basketball stds., playground, spray pool, sandbox, ice-
skating, day camp, fieldhouse,
2 gymnasiums, combination
assembly hall, 2 clubrooms,
kitchen, senior citizen center, artcraft, art center.

Shabbona Park
6935 W. Addison St. (3600 N)
283-6787

2 athletic fields, baseball, 3 jr.
baseball, softball, football &
soccer, 2 la bocci, 5 tennis, volleyball, 4 horseshoes, multiple-use
paved area, playground, spray
pool, 2 sandboxes, ice-skating,
day camp, fieldhouse, natatorium,
gymnasium, assembly hall, 7 clubrooms, craft shop, kitchen, artcraft, drama, senior citizen center,
yoga.

Shamrock Playlot Park
1901-31 W. 100th St. (10000 S)

playground, sandbox.

Shedd Park
3660 W. 23rd St.
521-2476

multiple-use paved area, 4 basket-

ball stds., volleyball, playground,
spray pool, sandbox, day camp,
fieldhouse, gymnasium, assembly
hall, 4 clubrooms, kitchen.

Sheil Park
3505-19 N. Southport Ave. (1400 W)
929-3070

playground, chess/checker tables,
fieldhouse, gymnasium, combination assembly hall, 6 clubrooms,
craft shop, kitchen, drama, music,
yoga.

Sheridan Park
910 S. Aberdeen St. (1100 W)
294-4717

athletic field, 4 softball, football &
soccer, 2 handball, ice-skating,
day camp, fieldhouse,
gymnasium, assembly hall, 6 clubrooms, craft shop, senior citizen
center.

Sherman Park
1307 W. 52nd St.
268-8436

swimming pool, athletic field, 2
baseball, 4 jr. baseball, 2 football
& soccer, running track (6 lap), 7
tennis, 2 handball, 2 horseshoes, 5
volleyball, multiple-use paved
area, 5 basketball stds., 2 playgrounds, spray pool, 4 sandboxes,
2 ice-skating, bicycle path, fieldhouse, 2 gymnasiums, assembly
hall, 6 clubrooms, kitchen, artcraft, public library, art center.

CITY CENTER PARKS

Sherwood Park
5705 S. Shields Ave. (332 W)
324-8887

swimming pool, athletic field, baseball, 2 jr. baseball, softball, football & soccer, day camp, fieldhouse, gymnasium, 4 clubrooms, craft shop, kitchen, senior citizen center.

Simons Park
1640 N. Drake Ave. (3535 W)
252-8697

volleyball, playground, spray pool, sandbox, ice-skating, 2 basketball stds., day camp, fieldhouse, gymnasium, assembly hall, 4 clubrooms, kitchen, artcraft, drama.

65th & Woodlawn Playlot Park
6514 S. Woodlawn Ave. (1200 E)

basketball std., playground.

64th & Ellis Playlot Park
6406-16 S. Ellis Ave. (1000 E)

4 basketball stds., playground, volleyball, multiple-use paved area.

Skinner Park
1331 W. Monroe St. (100 S)

athletic field, jr. baseball, football & soccer, 2 horseshoes, multiple-use paved area, 4 basketball stds., 4 volleyball, playground, ice-skating, 2 softball, recreation building, clubroom.

Smith Park
2558 W. Grand Ave.
227-0020

swimming pool, athletic field, 2 baseball, jr. baseball, football & soccer, 2 multiple-use paved areas, 8 basketball stds., 2 volleyball, 2 playgrounds, spray pool, 2 sandboxes, 2 ice-skating, 2 tennis, 3 la bocci, recreation building, 2 clubrooms.

Smith Playground
9912 S. Princeton Ave. (300 W)
995-7689

2 jr. baseball, multiple-use paved area, 4 basketball stds., 4 volleyball, playground, sandbox, ice-skating, day camp, recreation building, clubroom, kitchen.

Snowberry Playlot Park
1851-57 W. Huron St. (700 N)

playground, spray pool.

South Lakeview Playlot Park
1300-20 W. Wolfram St. (2832 N)

multiple-use paved area, 4 basketball stds., volleyball, playground, spray pool, sandbox.

Spruce Playlot Park
E 54th St. & S. Blackstone Ave. (1437 E)

playground, sandbox.

Stanton Park

640 W. Scott St. (1230 N)

294-4733

baseball, 2 jr. baseball, 3 horse-shoes, 2 multiple-use paved areas, 8 basketball stds., 4 volleyball, playground, sandbox, ice-skating, day camp, fieldhouse, natatorium, 2 gymnasiums, 8 clubrooms, assembly hall, 2 kitchens, music.

Stars and Stripes Playground Park

W. 51st Pl. & S. Sayre Ave. (7000 W)

jr. baseball, 4 basketball stds., multiple-use paved area, sandbox, spray pool, playground.

Stateway Park

3658 S. State St.

538-1132

swimming pool, athletic field, baseball, jr. baseball, 2 softball, football & soccer, multiple-use paved area, 4 basketball stds., 4 volleyball, spray pool, day camp, gymnasium, combination assembly hall, 3 clubrooms, art-craft, drama, music, art center.

CITY CENTER PARKS

Stony Island Park
E 88th St. & S. Clyde Ave. (2100 E)
221-6272

athletic field, baseball, 3 jr. baseball, football & soccer, 4 tennis, 4 horseshoes, multiple-use paved area, 4 basketball stds., 4 volleyball, playground, spray pool, sandbox, ice-skating, day camp, recreation building, club-room, artcraft.

Strohacker Park
4347 W. 54th St.
767-1933

athletic field, 3 softball, football & soccer, 2 horseshoes, 2 multiple-use paved areas, 6 basketball stds., volleyball, playground, spray pool, sandbox, 2 ice-skating, day camp, recreation building, clubroom.

Sumac Playlot Park
4201 S. Champlain Ave. (644 E)

multiple-use paved area, 2 basketball stds., playground, sandbox.

Summerdale Playlot Park
7262 W. Summerdale Ave. (5332 N)

playground, sandbox.

Sunflower Playlot Park
3442-46 W. Monroe St. (100 S)

playground, spray pool, sandbox.

Sun Yat Sen Playlot Park
W. 24th Pl. & S. Princeton Ave.
(300 W)

playground.

Superior Playlot Park
2101 W. Superior St. (732 N)

playground.

Sycamore Playlot Park
5109 S. Greenwood Ave. (1100 E)

playground, sandbox.

Tarkington School Park
334 W. 71st St.
436-2044

2 athletic fields, 3 baseball, 9 softball, 3 football & soccer, running track (6 lap), 21 tennis, 5 volleyball, 4 shuffleboard, 8 horseshoes, 5 basketball stds., multiple-use paved area, 3 playgrounds, spray pool, 2 sandboxes, archery range, 3 ice-skating, 2 day camps, bicycle path, casting pool, fishing lagoon, golf course, (9 holes), special recreation program, 3 gymnasiums, fieldhouse, assembly hall, 9 clubrooms, kitchen, artcraft, music, drama, craft shop, senior citizen center, yoga.

Taylor Park
W. 47th St. & S. Federal St. (100 W)
285-3385

swimming pool, athletic field, baseball, 3 jr. baseball, 2 football & soccer, tennis, multiple-use paved area, 6 basketball stds., 4 volleyball, day camp, gymnasium, combination assembly hall, 6 clubrooms, craft shop, kitchen, drama, music, senior citizen center.

Taylor-Lauridsen Playground Park
647 W. Root St. (4134 S)
927-1764

athletic field, baseball, 2 jr. baseball, football & soccer, multiple-use paved area, 2 basketball stds., volleyball, playground, sandbox, 2 ice-skating, day camp, recreation building, 2 clubrooms.

13th Street Playlot Park
E. 36th Pl. & S. Wabash Ave.
(45 E)

softball, basketball std., playground.

36th Place Playlot Park
NW Cor. E. 36th Pl. & S. Wabash Ave. (45 E)

softball, basketball std., playground.

33rd Place Playground Park
1635 W. 33rd Pl.
523-9294

volleyball, basketball std., playground, spray pool, sandbox, ice-skating, recreation building, clubroom.

CITY CENTER PARKS

Throop Playground Park
4920 S. Throop St. (1300 W)
924-2442

2 multiple-use paved areas, volleyball, 6 basketball stds., playground, spray pool, sandbox, ice-
skating, day camp, horseshoes,
recreation building, clubroom.

Throop Playlot Park
1811 S. Throop St. (1300 W)

multiple-use paved area, 2 basketball stds., playground, spray pool,
sandbox.

Tilton Playground Park
305 N. Kostner Ave. (4400 W)
626-8759

jr. baseball, multiple-use paved
area, 2 basketball stds., volleyball,
playground, sandbox, ice-skating,
recreation building, clubroom.

Touhy Park
7348 N. Paulina St. (1700 W)
465-2474

athletic field, 3 softball, football &
soccer, 2 tennis, multiple-use
paved area, 2 basketball stds.,
volleyball, playground, sandbox,

ice-skating, day camp, recreation
building, 2 clubrooms, kitchen.

Touhy Park
2107 W. Monroe St. (100 S)
294-4739

jr. baseball, multiple-use paved
area, 4 basketball stds., 4 volleyball, playground, spray pool,
sandbox, ice-skating, day camp,
gymnasium, combination
assembly hall, 2 clubrooms,
kitchen, artcraft, recreation
building, clubroom, drama.

Trebes Park
2250 N. Clifton Ave. (1150 W)
348-1563

jr. baseball, 4 basketball stds.,
3 horseshoes, playground, day
camp, gymnasium, 7 clubrooms,
music.

Trumbull Park
2400 E. 105th St.
768-1434

swimming pool, athletic field,
baseball, jr. baseball, 3 softball,
football & soccer, running track (6
lap), 4 tennis, 8 horseshoes,
multiple-use paved area,
volleyball, 4 basketball stds., playground, spray pool, 3 sandboxes, 2
ice-skating, day camp, fieldhouse,
2 gymnasiums, combination
assembly hall, 7 clubrooms, 2
kitchens, senior citizen center.

Trumbull Playground Park
2410 S. Trumbull Ave. (3432 W)
762-2244

playground, sandbox, recreation
building, clubroom.

Tuley Park
501 E. 90th Pl.
723-0150

swimming pool, athletic field, 2
baseball, 5 softball, football &
soccer, 13 tennis, 4 shuffleboard, 2
multiple-use paved areas, 8
basketball stds., volleyball, spray
pool, playground, 3 sandboxes, 2
ice-skating, day camp, fieldhouse,
2 gymnasiums, combination
assembly hall, 6 clubrooms, craft
shop, kitchen, artcraft, music,
drama, public library, senior
citizen center, yoga.

28th Place Playlot Park
W. 28th Pl. & S. Wallace St. (600
(600 W)

playground.

Union Park
1501 W. Randolph (150 N)
294-4738

swimming pool, athletic field,
baseball, 3 softball, football &
soccer, straightaway track (1 lap),
4 tennis, multiple-use paved area,
4 shuffleboard, 2 basketball stds.,
playground, spray pool, sandbox,
2 ice-skating, day camp, special

recreation program, fieldhouse, gymnasium, assembly hall, 5 clubrooms, drama, kitchen, artcraft.

Valley Forge Park
7001-7131 W. 59th St.

athletic field, 2 jr. baseball, 2 multiple-use paved areas, 4 basketball stds., 2 volleyball, 3 shuffleboard, 3 horseshoes, playground, sandbox.

Veterans' Memorial Playground Park
2820 E. 98th St.
221-6629

athletic field, baseball, 3 jr. baseball, football & soccer, multiple-use paved area, 2 basketball stds., volleyball, playground, spray pool, sandbox, ice-skating, day camp, recreation building, 2 clubrooms.

Violet Playlot Park
4120-38 W. Taylor St. (1000 S)

playground, spray pool.

Vittum Park
5033 W. 49th St.
735-8557
School Park
4950 S. LaPorte Ave. (4932 W)
735-8646

athletic field, baseball, 3 jr. baseball, football & soccer, 4 tennis, multiple-use paved area,

2 basketball stds., volleyball, playground, 2 ice-skating, day camp, sandbox, gymnasium, 6 clubrooms, recreation building, clubroom, artcraft.

Vogle Playlot Park
2100 W. Lawrence Ave. (4800 N)

playground.

Wagner Playlot Park
948 W. 51st St.
538-6220

2 softball, playground, spray pool, day camp.

Wallace Playground Park
607 W. 92nd St.
846-7346

softball, playground, spray pool, sandbox, volleyball, recreation building, clubroom.

Waller Public Bath
19 S. Peoria St. (900 W)

public bath building.

Walnut Playlot Park
3801-07 W. 45th St.

multiple-use paved area, 2 basketball stds., playground, sandbox.

Walsh Playground Park
1722-58 N. Ashland Ave. (1600 W)

multiple-use paved area, 4 basketball stds., playground, sandbox, spray pool.

Warren Park
2045 W. Pratt Ave. (6800 N)
465-0706

2 ice-skating.

Warren Playlot Park
2048 W. Warren Blvd. (34 N)

2 basketball stds., playground,
sandbox.

Washington Park
5531 S. King Dr. (400 E)
684-6530
Dyett Fieldhouse—513 E. 51st St.
548-1816
Special Recreation Program
752-2130

regional adventure playground,
swimming pool, athletic field, 6
baseball, 2 jr. baseball, 6 softball,
4 football & soccer, 14 tennis, 4
horseshoes, 5 shuffleboard,
volleyball, 8 multiple-use paved
areas, 18 basketball stds., 2
bowling greens, 4 playgrounds,
spray pool, 4 sandboxes, 2 day
camps, bicycle path, bridle path,
casting pool, archery range,
fishing lagoon, special recreation
program, fieldhouse, 4 gymnasiums, combination assembly
hall, 10 clubrooms, craft shop,
2 kitchens, artcraft, camera club,
lapidary shop, drama, music,
enameling, senior citizen center,
ceramics, artcraft, handball, yoga.

CITY CENTER PARKS

Washington Square Park
W. Walton St. & N. Clark St.
(932 N & 100 W)

passive recreation area, chess/
checker tables.

Washtenaw Playground Park
2521 S. Washtenaw Ave. (2700 W)
247-5499

softball, playground, spray pool,
sandbox, ice-skating, recreation
building, clubroom.

Washtenaw Playlot Park
2941 N. Washtenaw Ave. (2700 W)

playground, sandbox.

Welles Park
2333 W. Sunnyside Ave. (4500 N)
561-1184

athletic field, baseball, 3 jr. baseball, football & soccer, 3 tennis,
10 horseshoes, multiple-use paved
area, 4 shuffleboard, 4 basketball
stds., playground, 2 ice-skating,
day camp, special recreation
program, chess/checker tables,
fieldhouse, natatorium,
gymnasium, 4 clubrooms, craft
shop, kitchen, artcraft, senior
citizen center, yoga.

Wentworth Gardens Park
3770 S. Wentworth Ave. (200 W)
538-3995

swimming pool, jr. baseball, 3

basketball stds., 4 clubrooms,
kitchen, music, artcraft.

Wentworth Park
5625 S. Mobile Ave. (6300 W)
School Park—6325 W. 56th St.
585-1881

athletic field, 2 baseball, jr. baseball, football & soccer, 4 tennis,
multiple-use paved area, 12
basketball stds., 4 volleyball,
playground, sandbox, day camp,
2 ice-skating, 2 gymnasiums,
combination assembly hall, 6 clubrooms, natatorium, recreation
building, music.

West Chatham Park
8223 S. Princeton Ave. (300 W)
488-3019

athletic field, baseball, 2 jr. baseball, 2 softball, football & soccer, 2
tennis, multiple-use paved area,
2 basketball stds., volleyball,
straightaway track (1 lap), playground, spray pool, 2 ice-skating,
day camp, recreation building,
clubroom.

West End Playlot Park
4100 W. West End Ave. (160 N)

playground.

West Lawn Park
4233 W. 65th St.
582-6850

athletic field, baseball, 4 jr. baseball, football & soccer, 2 tennis, multiple-use paved area, 6 basketball stds., volleyball, playground, spray pool, 2 ice-skating, day camp, sandbox, fieldhouse, gymnasium, combination assembly hall, 6 clubrooms, arts and crafts room, 2 handball, kitchen, senior citizen center, music, craft shop, yoga.

West Pullman Park
W. 123rd St. & S. Stewart Ave. (400 W)
785-6963, 928-3233

athletic field, baseball, 2 jr. baseball, softball, football & soccer, 5 tennis, multiple-use paved area, 4 basketball stds., volleyball, 4 horseshoes, playground, spray pool, sandbox, 2 ice-skating, day camp, special recreation program, fieldhouse, natatorium, 2 gymnasiums, combination assembly hall, 6 clubrooms, craft shop, 2 kitchens, artcraft, yoga.

Western Playlot Park
907-17 N. Western Ave. (2400 W)

playground, sandbox.

White Park
1120 W. 122nd St.
785-6767

day camp, athletic field, 3 jr. base-ball, football & soccer, multiple-use paved area, 4 basketball stds., 2 tennis, playground, 2 ice-skating, fieldhouse, gymnasium.

Wicker Park
N. Damen Ave. & W. Schiller St. (2000 W & 1400 N)
276-7374

athletic field, baseball, 2 jr. baseball, football & soccer, 2 tennis, multiple-use paved area, 4 basketball stds., 4 volleyball, 2 shuffleboard, playground, spray pool, ice-skating, day camp, sand-box, gymnasium, combination assembly hall, 6 clubrooms, recreation building, artcraft.

Wildwood Park
(Wildwood Elem. Sch.)
6950 N. Hiawatha Ave. (6000 W)
631-7374

athletic field, baseball, 2 jr. baseball, football & soccer, 2 tennis, multiple-use paved area, 4 basketball stds., 4 volleyball, 2 shuffleboard, playground, spray pool, ice-skating.
    Joint operation with B. of E.— gymnasiums, comb. assembly hall, 6 clubrooms, recreation building, clubroom, art craft.

Williams Park
2830 S. State St.
294-4730
Williams School Park
2710 S. Dearborn St.
294-4730

athletic field, baseball, jr. baseball, 2 softball, football & soccer, 2 horseshoes, shuffleboard, multiple-use paved area, 4 basketball stds., 4 volleyball, spray pool, ice-skating, gymnasium, assembly hall, 5 clubrooms, kitchen, music, recreation building, artcraft.

Willow Playlot Park
E. 54th Pl. & S. Drexel Ave. (900 E)

playground, sandbox, spray pool.

Wilson Community Center Park
3225 S. Racine Ave. (1200 W)
523-2314

day camp, fieldhouse, gymnasium.

Wilson Park
4630 N. Milwaukee Ave. (5200 W)
545-7649

athletic field, jr. baseball, softball, football & soccer, 4 tennis, volleyball, 2 basketball stds., playground, sandbox, 2 ice-skating, day camp, fieldhouse, assembly hall, 7 clubrooms, 2 kitchens, artcraft, yoga.

Wilson Playground Park
1122 W. 34th Pl.
927-5786

basketball std., playground, spray pool, sandbox, ice-skating, recreation building, clubroom.

Winterberry Playlot Park
1211 W. Grand Ave. (530 N)

playground.

Witchhazel Playlot Park
711-19 W. 60th Pl.

playground.

Wolfe Playground Park
3325 E. 108th St.
721-4424

athletic field, baseball, football & soccer, multiple-use paved area, 2 basketball stds., volleyball, playground, spray pool, ice-skating, sandbox, day camp, recreation building, 2 clubrooms.

Woodhull Playground Park
7340 S. East End Ave. (1700 E)
493-8687

2 softball, multiple-use paved area, 2 basketball stds., playground, spray pool, sandbox, ice-skating, recreation building, 2 clubrooms.

Woodlawn Playlot Park
7420 S. Woodlawn Ave. (1200 E)

playground, sandbox.

CITY CENTER PARKS

Wrightwood Playground Park
2534 N. Greenview Ave. (1500 W)
549-7156

swimming pool, athletic field, football & soccer, running track (8 lap), 2 multiple-use paved areas, 8 basketball stds., playground, spray pool, ice-skating, sandbox, day camp, recreation building, clubroom.

Wrightwood Playlot Park
745 W. Wrightwood Ave. (2600 N)

playground, spray pool.

No. 276 Park
2021 N. Burling St. (735 W)
787-3274

softball, 4 basketball stds., day camp, gymnasium, 4 clubrooms.

No. 277 Park
E. 64th St. & S. Kenwood Ave. (1342 E)

jr. baseball, 2 tennis, 2 playgrounds, sandbox.

No. 278 Playground
E. 50th St. & S. Cottage Grove Ave.

multiple-use paved area, 4 basketball stds., 4 volleyball, playground.

No. 281 Playlot Park
E. 18th St. & S. Union Ave. (700 W)

6 basketball stds., shuffleboard, playground, spray pool, sandbox.

No. 284 Playlot Park
W. 26th St. & S. Stewart Ave. (400 W)

2 basketball stds., 2 volleyball, playground, sandbox.

No. 285 Park
W. Foster Ave. & N. Austin Ave. (5200 N & 6000 W)

jr. baseball, softball, playground, ice-skating.

No. 289 Park
E. 95th St. & S. Champlain Ave. (644 E)

2 jr. baseball, 2 tennis, 4 basketball stds., playground, spray pool, sandbox.

No. 291 Playground Park
E 54th Pl. & S. Greenwood Ave. (1100 E)

softball, 2 playgrounds, sandbox.

No. 293 Playlot Park
W. Drummond Pl. & N. Kimball Ave. (2632 N & 3400 W)

playground, sandbox.

No. 300 Park
E. 45th St. & S. Champlain Ave. (644 E)

swimming pool.

No. 302 Park
851 W. Waveland Ave. (3700 N)

swimming pool.

No. 303 Park
8914 S. Buffalo Ave. (3300 E)

swimming pool.

No. 309 Park
W. 57th St. & S. St. Louis Ave.
(3500 W)

jr. baseball, playground, ice-
skating, sandbox, day camp.

No. 310 Park
W. 40th St. & S. Federal St. (61 W)

swimming pool.

No. 311 Park
W. 53rd St. & S. Federal St. (61 W)

swimming pool.

No. 312 Park
W. 44th St. & S. Federal St. (61 W)

swimming pool.

No. 313 Park
2515 W. Jackson Blvd. (300 S)

swimming pool.

No. 314 Park
E. 132nd St. & S. St. Lawrence
Ave.

swimming pool.

No. 315 Park
W. Oak St. & N. Sedgwick Ave.
(1000 N & 400 W)

swimming pool.

CITY CENTER PARKS

No. 316 Park
W. Oakdale Ave. & N. Leavitt St.
(2932 N & 2200 W)

swimming pool.

No. 317 Park
5000 S. Union Ave. (700 W)

swimming pool.

No. 318 Park
1411 E. 62nd Pl.

swimming pool.

No. 319 Park
W. Walton St. & N. Wood St.
(930 N & 1800 W)

swimming pool.

No. 326 Playlot Park
6430-32 S. Kenwood Ave. (1332 E)

playground, spray pool.

No. 328 Playlot Park
6156 S. Dorchester Ave. (1400 E)

playground, spray pool.

No. 329 Playlot Park
6310-12 S. Drexel Ave. (900 E)

playground, spray pool.

No. 330 Playlot Park
6331-47 S. Harper Ave. (1500 E)

3 multiple-use paved areas, tennis,
volleyball, 8 basketball stds.

No. 331 Playlot Park
6600-04 S. Woodlawn Ave.
(1200 E)

playground, sandbox.

No. 335 Park
6525 N. Hiawatha Ave. (5200 W)
792-2127

athletic field, 3 softball, football &
soccer, 4 basketball stds., 3
volleyball, playground,
ice-skating, day camp,
gymnasium, combination
assembly hall, 4 clubrooms,
kitchen, artcraft, drama, music.

No. 337 Playlot Park
6446 S. Kimbark Ave. (1300 E)

playground, sandbox.

No. 350 Park
1830 S. Keeler Ave. (4200 W)

swimming pool.

No. 354 Playlot Park
7334-38 S. Maryland Ave. (832 E)

2 multiple-use paved areas, 4
basketball stds., volleyball.

No. 359 Playlot Park
1516-18 S. Karlov Ave. (4100 W)

playground, spray pool.

No. 360 Playlot Park
E. 18th St. & S. State St.

playground, sandbox, 2 basketball stds., volleyball.

No. 363 Park
9400 S. Greenwood Ave. (1100 E)

multiple-use paved area, spray pool, sandbox.

No. 373 Park
W. 115th St. & S. Homewood Ave. (1800 W)

athletic field, jr. baseball, football & soccer, multiple-use paved area, 4 basketball stds., volleyball, playground, chess/checker tables.

No. 386 Park
8385 S. Birkhoff Ave. (647 W)

2 jr. baseball, 2 multiple-use paved areas, 8 basketball stds., 2 tennis, Morgan Fieldhouse, gymnasium, combination assembly hall.

No. 390 Playlot Park
6340 N. Lakewood Ave. (1300 W)

playground.

No. 395 Playlot Park
7526-46 S. Lowe Ave. (632 W)

multiple-use paved area, 4 basketball stds., playground.

No. 396 Playlot Park
534-38 N. Albany Ave. (3100 W)

playground.

No. 397 Playlot Park
8421-29 S. Morgan St. (1000 W)

playground, sandbox.

No. 403 Playlot Park
6551-53 S. Wolcott Ave. (1900 W)

playground.

No. 404 Playlot Park
4956-58 S. Laflin St. (1500 W)

playground, spray pool.

No. 405 Playlot Park
1126-42 E. 80th St.

playground.

No. 406 Park
2334 W. Division St. (1200 N)
227-8565

athletic field, 2 jr. baseball, football & soccer, 2 tennis, day camp, Clemente Fieldhouse, natatorium, 2 gymnasiums.

No. 407 Park
744 N. Pulaski Rd. (4000 W)
826-3713

athletic field, 2 jr. baseball, football & soccer, straightaway track (1 lap), 3 tennis, 2 multiple-use paved areas, 8 basketball

CITY CENTER PARKS

stds., day camp, Orr Fieldhouse, natatorium, 2 gymnasiums.

No. 408 Park
4959 S. Archer Ave. (4000 W)
581-3230

athletic field, 4 jr. baseball, football & soccer, 2 multiple-use paved areas, 4 basketball stds., 5 tennis, day camp, volleyball, Curie Fieldhouse, natatorium, 2 gymnasiums, music, senior citizen center, yoga.

No. 409 Playground Park
S. Laramie Ave. & W. Harrison St. (5200 W & 600 S)-

jr. baseball.

No. 410 Playground Park
W. 56th St. & S. Lowe Ave. (632 W)

athletic field, 2 jr. baseball, football & soccer, 2 multiple-use paved areas, 8 basketball stds.

No. 411 Playlot Park
4220-30 N. Broadway (852 W)

playground.

No. 413 Playlot Park
240-44 N. Waller Ave. (5700 W)

playground.

No. 415 Playlot Park
345-51 W. 64th St.

playground.

No. 417 Playlot Park
5949-51 W. Huron St. (700 N)

playground.

No. 420 Playlot Park
5550-58 N. Magnolia Ave. (1224 W)

4 basketball stds.

No. 422 Playlot Park
S. Kedzie Ave. & W. Congress
Pkwy. (3200 W & 500 S)

playground, sandbox, spray pool.

No. 424 Playlot Park
4706-08 N. Pulaski Rd. (4000 W)

playground.

No. 425 Playlot Park
2645-59 N. Sheffield Ave. (1000 W)

playground, chess/checker tables.

No. 429 Park
7059 S. South Shore Dr. (2400 E)
363-2255

9-hole golf course, beach, 7
tennis, bowling green, playground,
fieldhouse, drama, senior citizen
center, artcraft, yoga.

No. 430 Playlot Park
650-52 N. Leamington Ave. (5132
W)

playground.

No. 435 Playlot Park
5400 N. Broadway (1200 W)

playground, chess/checker tables.

No. 438 Park
E. 130th St. & Calumet Expwy.

athletic field, 2 jr. baseball,
softball, football & soccer, running
track, 3 tennis, 6 multiple-use
paved areas, 12 basketball stds.

No. 442 Park
210 S. Loomis St. (1400 W)

athletic field, football & soccer,
4 tennis, 2 multiple-use paved
areas, 8 basketball stds., Young
Fieldhouse, natatorium, 2
gymnasiums, 4 clubrooms.

No. 445 Park
6918 W. Strong St. (4900 N)
631-2979

gymnasium, clubroom.

PASSIVE RECREATION AREAS

These city-owned parks are not for the active use of visitors; they simply are places where one can relax, sit down, gather with friends, or get involved with a good book.

Adams Park
7535-59 Dobson Ave. (1026 E)

Almond Park
W. 115th St. & Bell Ave. (2234 W)

Arcade Park
11132-56 S. St. Lawrence Ave.
(600 E)

Belden Triangle Park
401 W. Belden Ave. (2300 N)

Bickerdike Square Park
W. Ohio, N. Bishop & N. Armour
Streets (600 N-1438 W)

Bohn Park
1966-88 W. 111th St.

Buffalo Park
W. Sunnyside & N. California
Aves. (4500 N-2800 W)

Centennial Park
6068-6102 N. Northwest Highway
(6832 W)

Chamberlain Triangle Park
4227-37 S. Greenwood Ave.
(1100 E)

Connors Park
861-881 N. Wabash Ave. (45 E)

Eugenie Triangle Park
1701-11 N. LaSalle St. (150 W)

Fernwood Parkway Park
9501-10259 S. Eggleston Ave.
(432 W)

Hodes Park
1601-11 E. 73rd St.

Kinzie Parkway Park
W. Kinzie St., N. Laramie to N.
Long Aves. (400 N-5200 W)

Mariano Park
N. State St., E. Bellevue Pl. &
N. Rush St. (1031 N-1 E)

Merchants Park
W. Addison St. & N. Milwaukee
Ave. (3600 N-4200 W)

Mulberry Point Park
5865-79 N. Nina Ave. (7018 W)

Myrtle Grove Park
6101-25 N. Neva Ave. (7132 W)

Navy Pier Park
N. Lake Shore Dr. & E. Ohio St.
(600 N-485 E)

Normal Park
6701-6856 S. Lowe Ave. (632 W)

Norwood Circle Park
7101-31 W. Peterson Ave. (6000 N)

108th Place Triangle Park
W. 108th Pl. & S. Hoyne Ave.
(2100 W)

110th Place Triangle Park
W. 110th Pl. & S. Longwood Dr.
(2035 W)

112th Street Triangle Park
2234 W. 112th St.

116th Place Triangle Park
W. 116th Pl. & S. Bell Ave.
(2234 W)

118th Street Triangle Park
W. 118th St. & S. Bell Ave.
(2234 W)

Pleasant Parkway Park
1858-1930 W. 91st St. (9130 S)

Prospect Park
10940-11000 S. Prospect Ave. (1826
W.)

Prospect Point Park
W. 91st St. & S. Prospect Ave
(2050 W)

Pullman Park
11101-25 S. Cottage Grove Ave.
(501 E)

Ravenswood Manor Park
4604-46 N. Manor Ave. (2900 W)

Rutherford Park
2139-2219 N. Newland Ave. (6932
W)

Sunken Gardens Park
W. Sunnyside & N. Virginia Aves.
(4500 N-2650 W)

Wayne Park
W. Schreiber Ave., N. Ashland
Ave. to N. Clark St. (64232 N-
1600 W)

No. 444 Park
South bank of Chicago River
between N. Wabash & N. Dearborn
St. (300 N-36 W)

CHICAGO PARK DISTRICT
SPECIAL EVENTS AND ACTIVITIES

In addition to providing recreational facilities, the Chicago Park District sponsors many special seasonal events and activities. We have compiled a list based on 1978 activities; it is likely that these programs will continue to expand as your participation and interest increase.

For additional information, call your local park or the Park District Public Information Office (294-2490).

January
Indoor golf instruction, scuba diving lessons, ski instruction

February
Azalea & Camellia Flower Show (Garfield and Lincoln Park Conservatories), Children's Drama Festival, golf lessons

March
Indoor tennis instruction for beginners, floor hockey area play-offs, citywide boxing tournament, men's water polo tournament, swim meet (indoor)

100

April

Easter egg hunts, Park District Festival of Arts, area trials for the Special Olympics, kite-flying contests, floor hockey championship tournament, girls' and women's volleyball championship tournaments, opening of golf courses, indoor swimming club championships, beginning of smelt fishing, lagoon fishing

May

Chicago Sting soccer (Soldier Field), opening of Coho fishing contest, registration for day camps, Grant Park "Blossom Time", conclusion of smelt fishing, opening of boating season, Buckingham Fountain operation, fishing in park lagoons

June

Grant Park concerts, Theater on the Lake, opening of beaches, Chicago Sting soccer, Buckingham Fountain, lagoon fishing, sailing lessons (Rainbow Fleet)

July

Grant Park concerts, Theater on the Lake, Chicago Sting soccer, Buckingham Fountain, lagoon fishing, Chicago Park Special Olympics, sailing lessons, outdoor community concerts

August

Grant Park concerts, lagoon fishing, Buckingham Fountain, Theater on the Lake, Chicago Bears football (Soldier Field), Youth Parade, speed skating finals, North Avenue Beach swim, Chicago Lakefront Festival, All-Star Boxing Show, closing of outdoor pools (August 31), sailing lessons, outdoor community concerts

September

Bears football, lagoon fishing, end of sailing lessons, outdoor community concerts

October

Lagoon fishing, Bears football

November

Chrysanthemum Show (Lincoln and Garfield Park Conservatories), Bears football, public high school football semifinals and championship games (Soldier Field), Catholic high school football championship (Soldier Field)

December

Christmas Flower Show (Lincoln and Garfield Park Conservatories), Bears football, city championship football game (Soldier Field), Lincoln Park Theater

Created in 1915 "for the education, pleasure and recreation of the public," the Cook County Forest Preserve District has since fulfilled these aims to a great extent. Comprising a green belt around Chicago, the preserves are sanctuaries of native landscape with places for appropriate kinds of outdoor recreation along the fringes. The most popular form of recreation is picnicking, and the District provides over 2,200 such areas. Of these sites, 180 are designated for group picnics of 25 or more; permits must be obtained for these groups by personally visiting the Forest Preserve Picnic Permit Office in Room 230, County Building, 118 N. Clark Street, Chicago (443-6580).

For the cold-weather sports enthusiast, the District has 11 designated coasting and sledding areas, nine snowmobiling areas, and 16 toboggan slides at five locations. Each snowmobile must be registered with the District for a $5.00 fee. Toboggans can be rented at Jensen Slides and Swallow Cliff. Cross-country skiing is permitted upon any trail or open area (except special-use areas such as golf courses and nature preserves), and ice skating and fishing are allowed on District waters with ice thickness of at least four inches.

In warmer weather, the problems and expense of transporting boats to Lake Michigan can be avoided by making use of forest preserve lakes and rivers. Motorboating is permitted on the Calumet and Des Plaines Rivers; canoeing, rowboating and sailboating can be enjoyed on these rivers and on nine lakes. Certain lakes also offer rowboat rental. State rules and regulations govern fishing in Preserve waters; a valid hook and line license is required for everyone except those who are disabled, blind, or under 16 or over 65 years of age. Bow and arrow fishing is prohibited. Depth contour maps of major water holdings in the 2,000-acre fishing system are available upon request from the District.

Throughout the Preserves are facilities for more active physical recreation. Nearly 50 miles of bicycle trails and 200 miles of hiking and horseback riding trails are available or under construction. Horses may be rented from private stables near the equestrian trails; a District rider's license is required. Although swimming is banned in District waters, there are three fine pools open daily from 1 to 10 p.m. during the

COOK COUNTY FOREST PRESERVES

summer. There is a small admission charge, but children under 12 (and over six) can swim free from 2:30 to 4:30 on Mondays, Wednesdays and Fridays. The District operates eight challenging and widely distributed golf courses throughout the county, along with two driving ranges. Senior citizens and youngsters 17 and under can obtain special cards that enable them to play at half-price Monday through Friday until 4:00 p.m., excluding holidays. Green fees are $3.00 for nine-hole courses, $4.00 for 18-hole courses, and $5.00 for the championship caliber Highland Woods course. Gas-operated carts are available at five of the courses at $10.00 for 18 holes, and each course has its own pro shop.

The Forest Preserve District also operates five nature centers, where one can view exhibits and wildlife displays, and walk on self-guiding trails. Each center is different in terrain, exhibits and emphasis—all of which helps to foster appreciation of Cook County's natural features. Picknicking is not permitted at the Centers, but there are areas nearby for this purpose. Groups must make reservations by contacting the District's headquarters. Other special facilities of the Preserves include Brookfield Zoo, the Botanic Garden, nine model airplane flying fields, two model watercraft ponds, and seven overnight camping areas for properly supervised youth groups. There are no facilities for adult or trailer camping.

The District is divided into eleven divisions; descriptions of each will follow. For further information, contact the Division nearest you or the Forest Preserve Central Headquarters at 536 N. Harlem Avenue, River Forest, phone numbers 261-8400 (city) and 366-9420 (suburban).

FOREST PRESERVE ADDRESSES AND PHONE NUMBERS

NORTH
Des Plaines Division
801 N. River Rd., Mt. Prospect
824-1900

North Branch Division
6633 Harts Rd., Niles 775-4060

Northwest Division
I-90 E. Frontage Rd., ¾ mile N. of
Higgins, Palatine (no maps
available) 437-8330

Skokie Division
N. of Willow Rd., E. of Edens
X-way, Northfield 446-5652

CENTRAL
General H.Q.
536 N. Harlem, River Forest
261-8400

Indian Boundary Division
8800 W. Belmont,
Chicago 625-0606

Salt Creek Division
17th and Salt Creek, N. Riverside
485-8410

Picnic Permit Office
Rm. 230, County Bldg., 118 N.
Clark, Chicago 443-6580

SOUTH
Calumet Division
87th and Western, Chicago
233-3766

Palos Division
9900 S. Willow Springs Rd.,
Willow Springs 839-5617

Sag Valley Division
12201 McCarthy Rd., Palos Park
448-8532

Thorn Creek Division
Thornton-Lansing Rd., 1 mi. E. of
Thornton 474-1221

Tinley Creek
13800 S. Harlem, Orland Park
385-7650

Des Plaines Division

Points of Interest

1 Low dam with ramp for canoes and rowboats (shown at two locations

2 Gorgeous fall colors—Hard Maples (shown at five locations)

3 Methodist Camp Ground— typical of many such sites for annual gatherings owned and maintained by religious organizations

4 Site of Indian Village

5 Indian Trail Tree

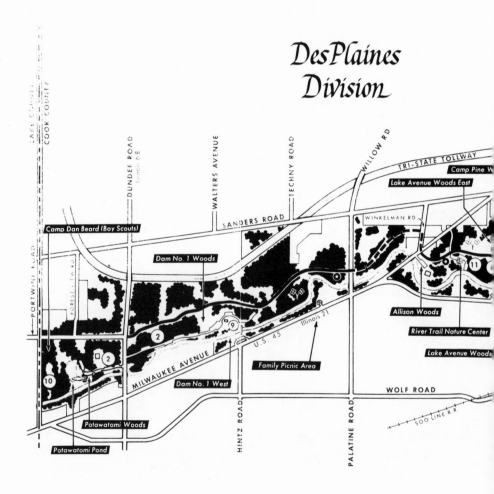

6 Dam No. 2—Large Weeping Willows on river banks
7 Site of Pioneer Cabin—Huge Cottonwoods—scenic area
8 Indian Portage to North Branch of Chicago River
9 Dam No. 1—scenic area

10 Indian Charcoal pits (Chipping Station)
11 River Trail Nature Center
12 Youth Group Camp (by permit only)

Division Phone Number: 824-1900

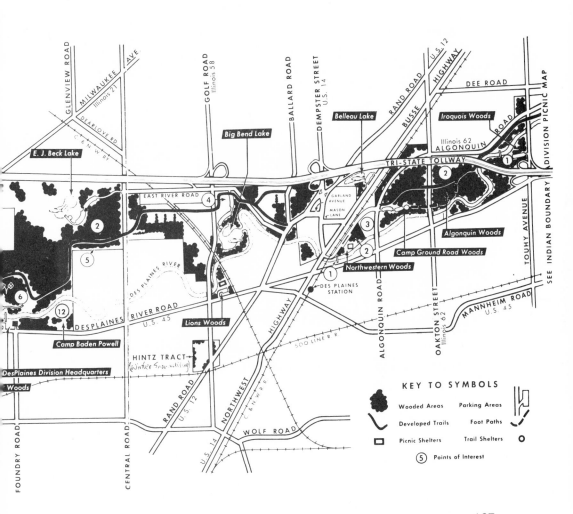

KEY TO SYMBOLS

Wooded Areas   Parking Areas

Developed Trails   Foot Paths

Picnic Shelters   Trail Shelters

⑤ Points of Interest

North Branch Division

Points of Interest

1. Charles "Chick" Evans, Jr.
   Golf Course (Skokie Division)
2. North Branch Division Headquarters (newly relocated in
   1958)
3. Jane (or Genevieve) Mirandeau
   Reserve
4. Victoria Porthier Reserve
5. Billy Caldwell (the Sauganash)
   Reserve
6. Edgebrook Golf Course—
   18 hole
7. Area notable for fine Hack-
   berry trees
8. Billy Caldwell Golf Course—
   9 hole
9. Indian Boundary Line
10. Chris Jensen Toboggan Slides

Division Phone Number: 775-4060

North Branch Division

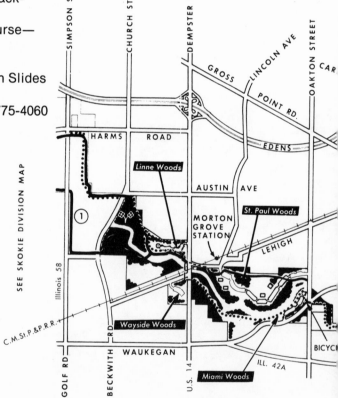

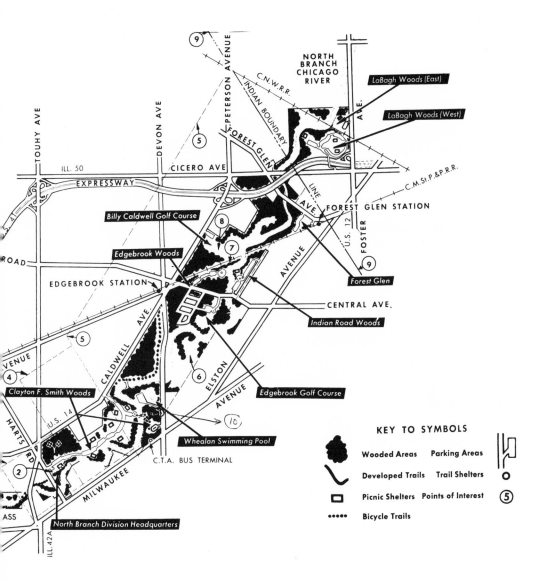

KEY TO SYMBOLS

Wooded Areas   Parking Areas

Developed Trails   Trail Shelters

Picnic Shelters   Points of Interest

Bicycle Trails

Northwest Division

Unfortunately, we cannot provide as much detail of the newly-organized Northwest Division of the Forest Preserve District as we'd like to. The Division contains some of the most outstanding features of the entire District, such as the Highland Woods Golf Course, Busse Lake, and the Crabtree Nature Center. We have included all the current information available; a comprehensive guide to the area should be forthcoming from the District within a few years.

Points of Interest

1 Crabtree Nature Center
2 Deer Grove Slides
3 Bode Lakes
4 Ned Brown Preserve
5 Busse Lake (within Ned Brown Preserve)
6 Highland Woods Golf Course
7 Spring Lake Nature Preserve
8 Shoe Factory Road Nature Preserve
9 Busse Forest Nature Preserve
10 Winter Snowmobiling Area—Northwest Field (½ mile east of Interstate 90 on Route 58, Elk Grove Village)

Division Phone Number: 437-8330

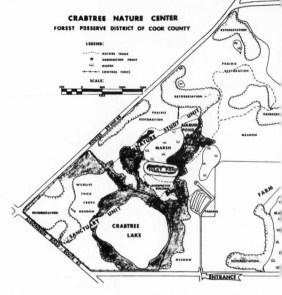

110

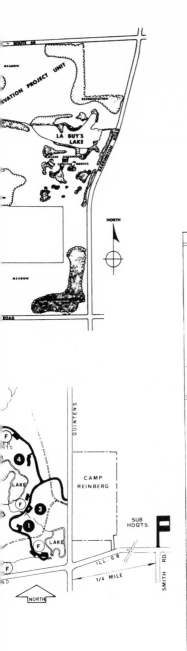

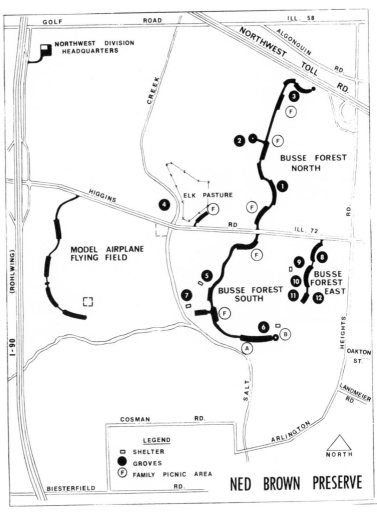

Skokie Division

Points of Interest

1 Sailboat Ramp
2 Skokie Division Headquarters
3 Charles "Chick" Evans, Jr.
18-hole golf course

4 Youth Group Camp (by permit only)

Division Phone Number: 446-5652

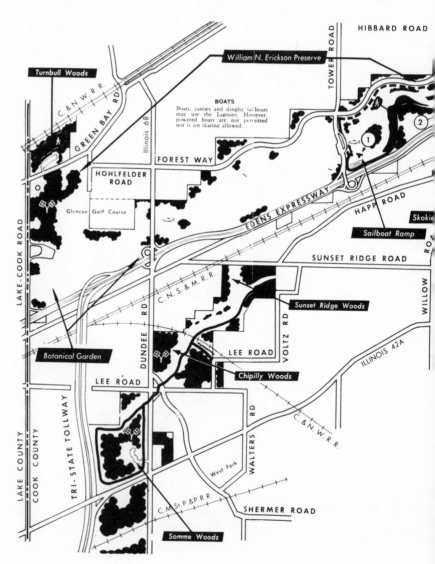

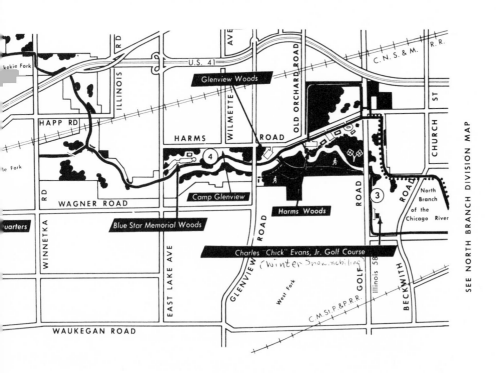

kokie Fork

U.S. 41

C.N.S. & M. R.R.

Glenview Woods

ILLINOIS RD

WILMETTE AVE

OLD ORCHARD ROAD

CHURCH ST

HAPP RD

HARMS ROAD

④

Camp Glenview

Harms Woods

le Fork

WAGNER ROAD

WINNETKA RD

③

North
Branch
of the
Chicago River

uarters

Blue Star Memorial Woods

EAST LAKE AVE

GLENVIEW ROAD

ROAD

ROAD

BECKWITH

SEE NORTH BRANCH DIVISION MAP

Charles "Chick" Evans, Jr. Golf Course

(Winter Snowmobiling)

West Fork

C.M.St.P.&P.R.R.

Illinois 58

GOLF

WAUKEGAN ROAD

Skokie Division

KEY TO SYMBOLS

Wooded Areas   Parking Areas

Developed Trails   Foot Paths

Picnic Shelters   Trail Shelters   O

..... Bicycle Trails   Points of Interest   ②

Indian Boundary Division

Points of Interest

1 Trailside Museum—exhibits of native animals
2 Lagoons for ice skating in winter and fishing in the summer
3 Evans Field—site of Indian Village and chipping station.

There were several Indian burial places and temporary villages along their main trail following the Des Plaines River. Just east of Evans Field, there were five mounds built by prehistoric Indians.

Indian Boundary Division

4 Indian Boundary Line—north line of a strip 20 miles wide from Lake Michigan to Ottawa ceded to the whites by the Potawatomi in 1816.

5 Park of La Framboise Reserve —granted to a half-breed Indian for aid to the whites at the Fort Dearborn massacre.

6 St. Joseph Cemetery—site of Indian Village

7 Model airplane flying field

8 Robinson Reserve—granted to Alexander Robinson (Chief Che-Che-Pin-Qua) for many years of aid to the whites

9 Indian Cemetery—graves of Chief Robinson and family

10 Low dam with ramp for canoes and rowboats (shown at two locations)

Division Phone Number: 625-0606

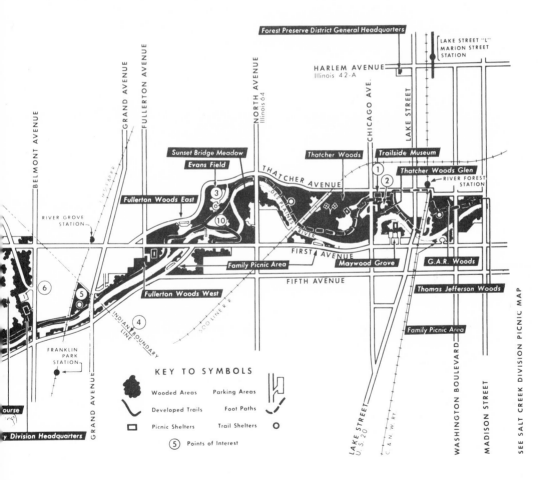

115

Salt Creek Division

Points of Interest

1 Forest Preserve District
 Nursery
2 Salt Creek Division Headquarters
3 Chicago Zoological Park
 (Brookfield Zoo)
4 Site of Checkerboard Flying
 Field—terminal for first
 commercial airmail service
5 Forest Preserve District central
 warehouse, shops and garage
6 Flying field for model airplanes
7 Hoffman Dam and Tower
8 Cermak Swimming Pool
9 Stony Ford
10 Laughton's Ford
11 Site of Laughton Trading Post
12 Catherine Mitchell Lagoon
13 The Chicago Portage—National
 Historic Site
14 Boat Launching Site
15 Togoggan slides and warming
 shelter

Division Phone Number: 485-8410

Salt Creek Division

116

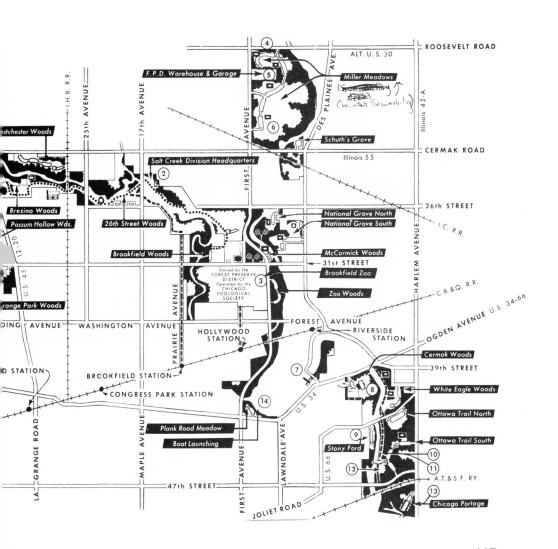

ROOSEVELT ROAD

ALT. U.S. 30

Miller Meadows

(Winter Snowmobiling)

F.P.D. Warehouse & Garage

Schuth's Grove

CERMAK ROAD

Illinois 55

Illinois 42-A

DES PLAINES AVE.

25th AVENUE

17th AVENUE

FIRST AVENUE

estchester Woods

Salt Creek Division Headquarters

26th STREET

National Grove North
National Grove South

Brezina Woods

Possum Hollow Wds.

26th Street Woods

Brookfield Woods

McCormick Woods

31st STREET

Owned by the
FOREST PRESERVE
DISTRICT
Operated by the
CHICAGO
ZOOLOGICAL
SOCIETY

Brookfield Zoo

Zoo Woods

r000 Park Woods

HARLEM AVENUE

I.C. R.R.

C.B.&Q. R.R.

OGDEN AVENUE U.S. 34-66

FOREST   AVENUE

DING   AVENUE   WASHINGTON   AVENUE

HOLLYWOOD
STATION

RIVERSIDE
STATION

Cermak Woods

39th STREET

White Eagle Woods

PRAIRIE   AVENUE

BROOKFIELD STATION

CONGRESS PARK STATION

Ottawa Trail North

Ottawa Trail South

U.S. 34

Plank Road Meadow

Boat Launching

Stony Ford

Ottawa Trail South

Chicago Portage

LA GRANGE ROAD

MAPLE AVENUE

FIRST AVENUE

LAWNDALE AVE.

U.S. 66

47th STREET

JOLIET ROAD

A.T.&S.F. RY.

I.H.B. R.R.

U.S. 45

12-20

④ ⑤ ⑥ ② ③ ⑦ ⑧ ⑨ ⑩ ⑪ ⑫ ⑬ ⑭

117

Calumet Division

Points of Interest

1 Boulder marking site of Indian signal station and camp ground overlooking Chicago Plain eastward and northward.
2 Calumet Division Headquarters
3 Indian Boundary Line
4 Thornton-Blue Island Road (Hubbard's Trail)
5 Model airplane flying field
6 Boat launching site
7 Pipe O'Peace Golf Course— 18-hole; winter snowmobiling
8 Eggers Grove, one of the few places in Cook County where sassafras trees are native.

9 Wolf Lake State Park and Conservation Area (See State Park section for details)
10 Powder Horn Lake
11 Burnham Woods Golf Course— 18-hole

Division Phone Number: 233-3766

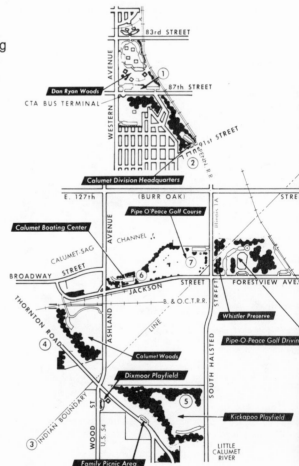

Calumet Division

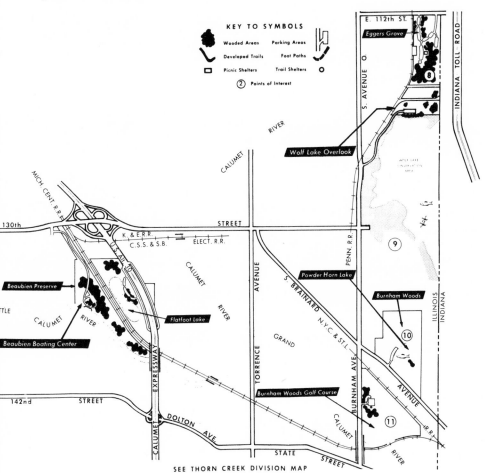

KEY TO SYMBOLS

Wooded Areas   Parking Areas
Developed Trails   Foot Paths
Picnic Shelters   Trail Shelters
② Points of Interest

E. 112th ST.

Eggers Grove

S. AVENUE O.

INDIANA TOLL ROAD

⑧

RIVER

CALUMET

Wolf Lake Overlook

WOLF LAKE CONSERVATION AREA

MICH. CENT. R.R.

130th

STREET

K. & E.R.R.
C.S.S. & S.B.   ELECT. R.R.

U.S. RT. 12

PENN. R.R.

⑨

ILLINOIS
INDIANA

Beaubien Preserve

CALUMET

CALUMET

RIVER

AVENUE

S. BRAINARD

Powder Horn Lake

Burnham Woods

⑩

LITTLE

CALUMET

RIVER

Flatfoot Lake

TORRENCE

GRAND

N.Y.C. & ST.L.

Beaubien Boating Center

CALUMET EXPRESSWAY

142nd   STREET

DOLTON   AVE.

Burnham Woods Golf Course

BURNHAM AVE.

AVENUE

⑪

R.R.

STATE   STREET

CALUMET

RIVER

SEE THORN CREEK DIVISION MAP

119

Palos and Sag Valley Divisions

Points of Interest

1 Palos Division Headquarters
2 Little Red Schoolhouse Nature Center and Trails
3 Old Country Lane
4 Maple Lake boat dock—rowboats for hire
5 Site of original Argonne Laboratory for atomic research
6 Abandoned golf course—good ski slopes—future shelter
7 Dynamite Road nature trails
8 St. James Church and Cemetery, founded in 1837. Site of Indian village, chipping station and signal station.
9 Camp Sagawau—Outdoor Education Center—no picnics allowed
10 Abandoned limestone quarry
11 Toboggan slides and shelter
12 Trail located on glacial ridge, called an esker
13 Trail through wild isolated area with fine scenery
14 Sag Valley Division Head-quarters
15 Model airplane flying field—winter snowmobiling

Division Phone Number: 839-5617

Forest Preserve District of Cook County
IN RELATION TO
The City of Chicago

Palos Division

Palos & Sag Valley Divisions

Sag Valley Division

120

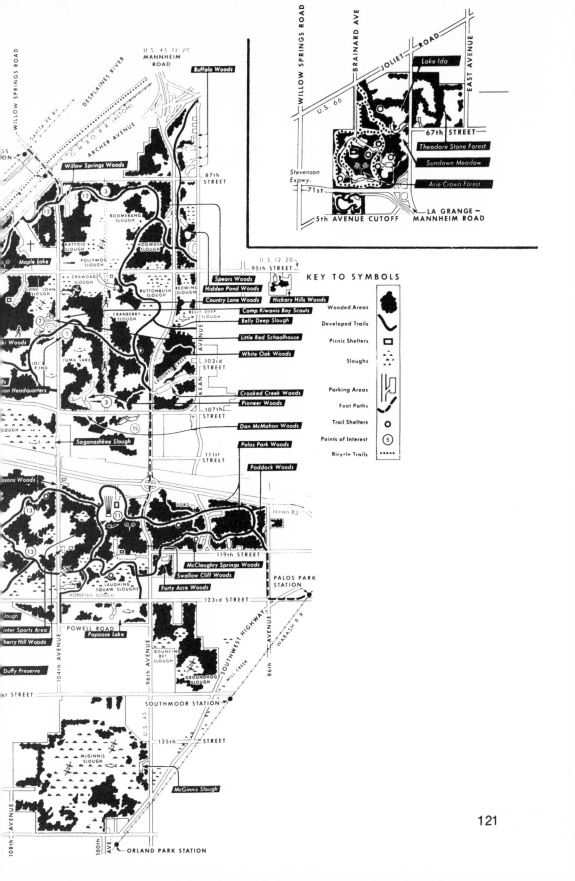

KEY TO SYMBOLS

Wooded Areas	
Developed Trails	
Picnic Shelters	
Sloughs	
Parking Areas	
Foot Paths	
Trail Shelters	
Points of Interest	
Bicycle Trails	

121

Thorn Creek Division

Points of Interest

1 Thorn Creek Division Headquarters
2 Thornton sewage treatment works
3 Green Lake, formerly a deep clay pit for making brick
4 Youth Group Camp (by permit only)—two sites

5 Sauk Trail Road—originally part of the Indian trail from the Mississippi River to Fort Dearborn
6 Pioneer homesite of John McCoy, soldier in the revolutionary War; a "station" on the "Underground Railroad" for escaped slaves.

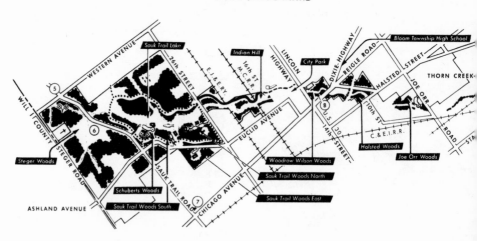

Thorn Creek Division

7 Brown's Corners—a crossroads of midwest America in
pioneer days—intersection of
the Great Sauk Trail with
Hubbard's Trace to Danville
and, later, Vincennes Road.
8 Site of Absalom Well's cabin—
first white settler in this part
of Cook County.

9 Thornton quarry, largest in
the Chicago region, notable for
fossils and a coral reef in
the Niagara limestone
10 Sand Ridge Nature Center

Division Phone Number: 474-1221

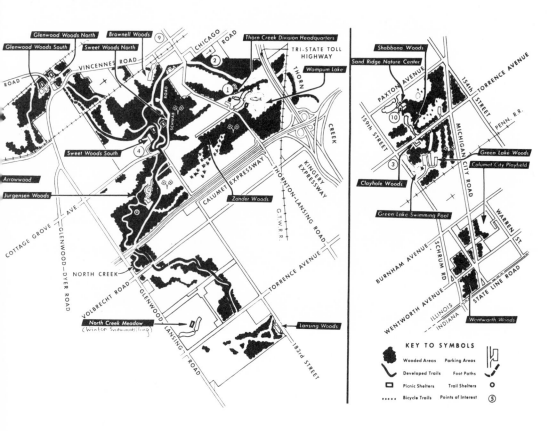

Tinley Creek Division

Points of Interest

1 Turtlehead Lake, one of several Forest Preserve lakes dug to provide earth fill for the Tri-State Tollway.
2 Deep ravines and gullies along Tinley Creek
3 Tinley Creek Division Headquarters

4 Tinley Creek Woods, notable for a few huge oaks surviving from the primeval forest in this region.
5 Camp Falcon, a camping center for youth groups by permit only
6 Camp Sullivan, a camping center for youth groups by permit only
7 Site of Goeselville, once a crossroads trading place and post office on the Midlothian Turnpike.

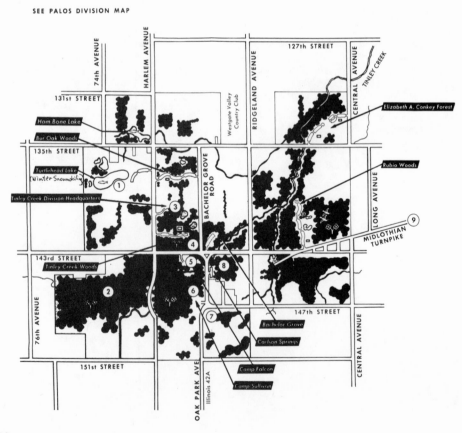

SEE PALOS DIVISION MAP

8 Carlson Springs, one of the few large springs now flowing in Cook County.

9 Midlothian Turnpike, originally an Indian trail and later a country road from Harlem Ave. and 151st St., through Goeselville to Blue Island

10 Oak Forest Hospital, Cook County institution for the indigent, aged and infirm.

11 Franciscan Monastery serving Oak Forest Hospital

12 Indian Boundary Line, beginning at a point on the shore of Lake Michigan, 10 miles south of the mouth of the Chicago River. South Boundary of a strip, 20 miles wide from Chicago to Ottawa, ceded by the Potawatomi and allied tribes in 1816.

Division Phone Number: 385-7650

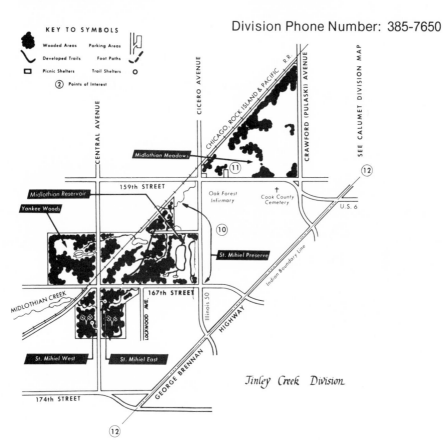

Tinley Creek Division

CHICAGO AREA NATURE PRESERVES

Not all outdoor recreation has to be concerned with athletic activity. It is often a good idea just to encounter our surroundings in their natural state, in order to better appreciate wonders not wrought by man. The Illinois Nature Preserves System provides such an opportunity by setting aside various areas of land and maintaining them in an undisturbed condition. Each preserve can be thought of as a living museum, preserving the habitats of rare native Illinois plants and animals, as well as exhibiting examples of all significant natural geographic features.

The nature preserves within the system are owned and managed by the Illinois Department of Conservation, the Cook County Forest Preserve District, the Nature Conservancy, and several other public and private groups. This guide includes only those preserves in northwestern Illinois. For further information contact:

Illinois Department of Conservation: (312) 793-2070

Nature Conservancy, 666 N. Lake Shore Dr., Chicago: (312) 787-1791

Illinois Nature Preserves Commission, 819 N. Main St., Rockford, Il 61103.

Admission is free, although advance permission is required to visit some preserves. A complete list of nature preserve rules and regulations is available from the Department of Conservation.

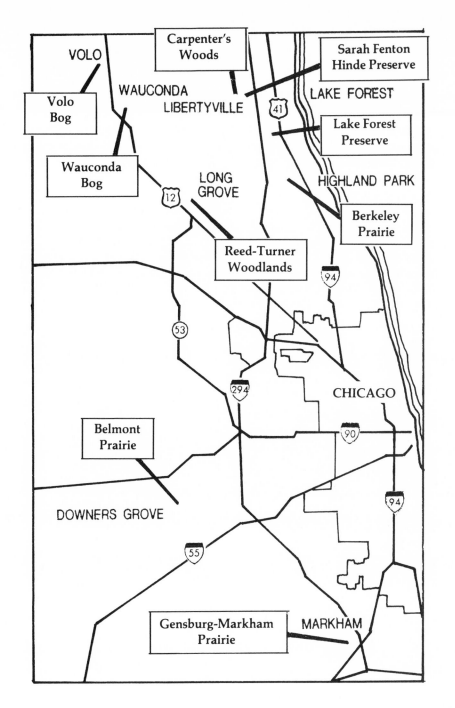

VOLO

Carpenter's
Woods

Sarah Fenton
Hinde Preserve

Volo
Bog

WAUCONDA
LIBERTYVILLE

LAKE FOREST

41

Lake Forest
Preserve

Wauconda
Bog

LONG
GROVE

12

HIGHLAND PARK

Berkeley
Prairie

Reed-Turner
Woodlands

94

53

294

CHICAGO

Belmont
Prairie

90

94

DOWNERS GROVE

55

Gensburg-Markham
Prairie

MARKHAM

NATURE PRESERVES IN AND AROUND CHICAGO

	Located in	Owned/Managed by
NORTH		
Berkeley Prairie	Highland Park Lake County	NC
Illinois Beach	North of Waukegan Lake County	IDC
Lake Forest	Lake Forest Lake County	NC
Edward Ryerson	NW of Riverwoods Lake County	IDC
NORTHWEST		
Busse Forest	Cook County	CCFP (NW Division)
Shoe Factory Road	Hanover Township Cook County	CCFP (NW Division)
Trout Park	Elgin Kane County	City of Elgin
Cedar Lake Bog	West of Lake Villa Lake County	IDC
Carpenter's Woods	Libertyville Lake County	NC
Sarah Fenton Hinde	Libertyville Lake County	NC
Pistakee Bog	Libertyville Lake County	IDC
Reed-Turner Woodlands	Long Grove Lake County	NC
Volo Bog	Volo Lake County	NC
Wauconda Bog	Wauconda Lake County	NC
Kettle Moraine	SE of McHenry McHenry County	IDC
Spring Lake	Cook County	CCFP

SOUTH

Gensburg-Markham Prairie	Markham Cook County	NC
Jurgenson Woods North	Cook County	CCFP (Thorn Creek Division)
Sand Ridge	Cook County	CCFP
Thornton-Lansing Road Zander Woods	Cook County	CCFP (Thorn Creek Division)

SOUTHWEST

Black Partridge Woods	Lemont Township Cook County	CCFP (Sag Valley Division)
Cap Sauer's Holdings	Palos & Lemont Tshps. Cook County	CCFP (Sag Valley Division)
Cranberry Slough	Palos Township Cook County	CCFP (Palos Division)
Paw Paw Woods	Palos Township Cook County	CCFP (Palos Division)
Goose Lake Prairie	East of Morris Grundy County	IDC

WEST

Salt Creek Woods	Cook County	CCFP (Salt Creek Division)
Belmont Prairie	Downers Grove DuPage County	NC

CCFP—Cook County Forest Preserve District
IDC—Illinois Department of Conservation
NC—Nature Conservancy

COOK COUNTY

Black Partridge Woods Nature Preserve

This preserve, which encompassess 80 acres, features river bluffs and forested ravines as well as a springfed stream and is located on the north side of Bluff Road northwest and across the Des Plaines River valley from Lemont. A parking area and trails are provided.

Busse Forest Nature Preserve

Four-hundred-forty acres in size, Busse Forest contains upland forest, marsh vegetation and an abundance of wild flowers and shrubs. The preserve is located north of Higgins Road (Route 72), between Salt Creek and the forest preserve entrance drive. Parking is available, and some trails are being developed.

Cap Sauer's Holdings Nature Preserve

Upland forest, marsh, intermittent streams, ponds, and moraine topography are represented in this large preserve of 1,520 acres. It is located west of 104th Avenue, south of Route 83 to Ford Road and McCarthy Road (123rd St.) Trails have been developed, and parking is available at Teason's Woods on the east side of 104th Avenue.

Cranberry Slough Nature Preserve

Cranberry Slough offers both a peat bog and upland forests, containing unusual plants and animals. The 400-acre preserve is located west of Mannheim Road (U.S. 45) and south of 95th Street. Trails are developed, and parking is available at Belly Deep Slough.

Gensburg-Markham Prairie Nature Preserve

This 120 acre preserve is a true virgin prairie, featuring over 200 plant species as well as rare animals. It is located in Markham, northeast of 159th Street (U.S. 6), on Kedzie Avenue. Advance permission to visit the preserve can be obtained by calling Dr. Robert Betz, Northeastern Illinois University, 583-4050 Ext. 704.

Jurgensen Woods North Nature Preserve

Jurgensen Woods is a 120 acre preserve with a wet-mesic oak forest within its expanses. It is located south of 183rd Street, east of forest preserve entrance drive and west of the Calumet Expressway. Parking is provided, and trails have been developed.

Paw-Paw Woods Nature Preserve
This 105-acre area contains some of the south bluff and floodplain of the Des Plaines River valley. The preserve is located on both sides of Archer Avenue, from 95th Street to the Gulf, Mobile and Ohio Railroad, and west of Fairmont Cemetery. No parking or trails have been developed.

Salt Creek Woods Nature Preserve
Upland forest, floodplain forest, small ponds and Salt Creek are featured in this 245-acre preserve, which is located south of 31st Street, east of Wolf Road, and north and west of Salt Creek. Parking is available at Bemis Woods, and trails are developed.

COOK COUNTY

Sand Ridge Nature Preserve
This 70-acre area consists of long ridges and low swales of lakeshore deposited sands, with various prairie wild flowers and grasses present. It is located east of Torrence Avenue, west of the Penn Central Railroad, north of Michigan City Road and south of Pulaski Road (134th Street). No parking or trails have been developed.

Shoe Factory Road Nature Preserve
This nine-acre preserve is a gravel hill prairie, accessible by permission of the naturalist at Crabtree Farm Nature Center. It is located on the south side of Shoe Factory Road, midway between Sulton Road (Route 59) and the Elgin, Joliet and Eastern Railroad, in Hanover Township.

Spring Lake Nature Preserve
A steep-sloped forest, extensive marshes, Spring Lake, and some mesic prairie are contained in this 560-acre preserve, bounded by Donlea Road, Cook-Lake County Line Road, Bateman Road, and Sulton Road. No parking or trails have been developed.

Thornton-Lansing Road Zanders Woods Nature Preserve
Unusual shrubs and wild flowers accent this 440-acre expanse of forest, sand prairie and marsh. It is located south of 183rd Street and Thorn Creek (Schwab) Road, south of Thornton-Lansing Road and west of the Calumet Expressway. Parking is available along Zanders Road, but no trails have been developed.

DU PAGE COUNTY

Belmont Prairie Nature Preserve
One of the last portions of Valparaiso Moraine prairie, this 9.8-acre preserve contains rare plants and is located at Haddow and Cross Streets in Downers Grove. Access can be obtained by calling Mr. or Mrs. Alfred Dupress, Belmont Prairie Preservation Society, 968-2040.

GRUNDY COUNTY

Goose Lake Prairie Nature Preserve
Within Goose Lake's 1,513 acres is contained the largest remnant of prairie in Illinois, complete with a wide array of uncommon wildlife and water fowl. It is located north of Lorenzo Road and east of Jugtown Road, about six miles east of Morris. Access is via a visitor center off Jugtown Road on the west side of the preserve. Trails are developed.

KANE COUNTY

Trout Park Nature Preserve
This 26-acre preserve features upland forest, seepage areas, springs, and glacial features of the Fox River bluffs. It is located on the northeast edge of the city of Elgin between Duncan Avenue and Dundee Avenue. south of the Northwest Tollway. Trout Park is owned by the City of Elgin, Parks and Recreation Department, and trails are laid out through the area. Parking is available.

LAKE COUNTY

Berkeley Prairie Nature Preserve
This 18-acre part-virgin prairie is located in Highland Park, just past the intersection of Berkeley and Ridge Roads. Advance permission to visit this preserve can be obtained by calling the Lake County Forest Preserve District, 367-6640.

Cedar Lake Bog Nature Preserve
This 27.5-acre area includes a youthful lakeside bog, an upland woods, a marsh, and a portion of a natural glacial lake. It is located along the west edge of Cedar Lake just west of Lake Villa. Access is via foot from Route 132 to the edge of the marsh; there is no boardwalk at present.

Carpenter's Woods and the Sarah Fenton Hinde Nature Preserve
Carpenter's Woods is a typical hardwood forest on the Des Plaines River flood plain; the Hinde Preserve is a 10.3-acre upland forest. The Nature Conservancy-owned preserves are managed by Lake Forest College. Permission to visit can be obtained from John Munshower, Lake Forest College Biology Department, 234-3100. The two areas are both located near Libertyville; Carpenter's Woods is north of St. Mary's Road on Old School Road, and the Hinde Preserve is south of St. Mary's Road on Everett Road.

Illinois Beach Nature Preserve
This 829-acre preserve includes beach, dunes, cattail marshes, and alternating sand ridges and swales. Located on Lake Michigan north of Waukegan, south of Illinois Beach State Park Lodge and east of the Chicago and Northwestern Railroad, it also provides excellent wildlife habitat and is an important refuge for migrating birds. Parking is provided just south of the Illinois Beach Lodge. An interpretive center and trails have been developed.

Lake Forest Preserve
This is a small but popular spot for students to study prairie remnants. Permission to visit can be obtained by calling Paul Ahern, Lake Forest Open Lands Association, 234-4072 or 822-9666.

Pistakee Bog Nature Preserve
This 88-acre preserve represents a later phase of bog succession to dry land, lacking any areas of open water. It is located 1.5 miles west of the junction of Illinois Route 134 and U.S. Route 12. Access has not been developed.

LAKE COUNTY

Reed-Turner Woodlands Nature Preserve
Upland deciduous forest, a ten-acre pond and a restored prairie field highlight this area. A variety of rare wild flowers and small animals are also included in this preserve, which is located about one-half mile south of the Old McHenry and Half Day Road (Illinois Route 22) intersection in Long Grove. Visiting permission is obtainable by calling Mrs. Harold Turner, 438-7230.

Edward L. Ryerson Nature Preserve
This 150-acre preserve includes many species of trees within its old growth forest along the Des Plaines River valley. It is located northwest of Riverwoods, between Riverwoods Road, Deerfield Road, and the Des Plaines River. The Lake County Forest Preserve District has developed parking, trails, and a nature center. Access is from Aptahisic Road.

Volo Bog Nature Preserve
Volo Bog is the only bog in Illinois that contains a well developed Tamarack forest and all prior stages of bog succession. The 161-acre area is located two miles northwest of Volo and may be reached by proceeding 1.2 miles north of Volo on U.S. 12, then 1.4 miles west on Sullivan Lake Road, then 0.3 miles north and east on Brandenburg Road. A parking area and trail are provided, and access is controlled by a watchman during the summer months.

Wauconda Bog Nature Preserve
This is a bog in the old-age stage of bog development that contains no open water areas. The 6.7-acre preserve also includes several species of rare plants and is located on the south side of the village of Wauconda, east of Rand Road. No access has been developed.

McHENRY COUNTY

Kettle Moraine Nature Preserve
This preserve consists of two tracts, which contain examples of marsh, fen, bog, and forest, as well as kettle moraine topography. The two tracts, covering 242 acres, are located within the McHenry Dam-Lake Defiance State Park, three miles southeast of McHenry. Nature trails and a boardwalk have been developed in this area.

ILLINOIS DEPARTMENT OF CONSERVATION
STATE PARKS AND CONSERVATION AREAS

In addition to the Cook County Forest Preserves system, the Illinois Department of Conservation has an extensive network of state parks and conservation areas. We have included only those areas near Chicago—for a full listing, contact the Illinois Department of Conservation, Information/Education Division, State Office Building, Springfield, Illinois, 62706 or call their Chicago office at 793-2070.

All state parks are open the year round. When weather conditions necessitate the closing of park roads, access to park facilities is by foot only. Groups of 25 or more persons must obtain permission from the site manager to use facilities; all pets must be on a leash.

William W. Powers Conservation Area

The William W. Powers Conservation Area is on Chicago's far southwest side, off highways 94, 90, and 41. The main park entrance is at 123rd Street and Avenue O. The area is 580 acres in size, 419 of which are water.

There is a large picnic area with a good number of tables and stoves located south of the main entrance, paralleling Avenue O. A shelter is available on a first-come basis. A concession stand is in the middle of the picnic area near a modern toilet facility building and drinking fountains. Rental boats are provided at the rear of the stand.

Wolf Lake contains numerous varieties of fish, and it has about six miles of shoreline available for bank fishermen. Boat fishing is also allowed, and a two-lane launching ramp has been provided north of the main entrance. Motors of ten horsepower or less are permitted. The area is used for waterfowl hunting during the fall of the year. Hunting must be done from authorized blinds, which are allocated on a two-year basis at a public drawing during the summer of even numbered years. Unoccupied blinds are available on a daily basis. Wolf Lake also is available for ice skating, ice fishing and ice boating, providing that the ice is thick enough.

Camping and swimming are not permitted in the Powers Area, which is open daily from sunrise to sunset. For more details about this site, contact Ranger, 12800 Avenue O, Chicago, Illinois, 60633; phone 312/646-3270.

Moraine Hills State Park

The Moraine Hills State Park is located in the northeast corner of Illinois, three miles south of McHenry, with the park entrance off River Road. The Fox River runs through the western portion of the 1,668-acre park, which consists of approximately 940 acres of uplands and 729 acres of wetlands, including four small lakes totaling 95 acres. The area features Leatherleaf Bog and Pike Marsh nature preserves, as well as Lake Defiance, one of the few natural glacial lakes in Illinois. McHenry Dam controls the water level in the Chain O'Lakes, and the adjoining lock operation allows pleasure boats and other craft to get around the dam and thus travel from Chain O'Lakes to Algonquin.

Picnic tables are provided throughout the eight major day use areas. Each area provides parking, drinking water and rustic outhouses equipped with septic tanks. Flush toilet facilities are provided at the park office and the McHenry Dam concession building, which provides refreshments and fishing gear. Private canoes and boats may be brought into the park by car top only, for use on the Fox River at the Dam area. Rental boats are available at the concession stand, and there is a 25 horsepower limit.

The use of private boats of any kind is prohibited on Lake Defiance, but a limited number of boats specifically for use on this lake can be reserved from the park office. Because of the extremely unstable pear soil shoreline, no bank fishing is allowed on Lake Defiance.

Fishing is permitted on the Fox River, and access to the river is provided at the McHenry Dam area. The northern lakes area—Tomahawk, Warrior and Wilderness lakes—provide bank fishing and carry-in car top boats (no motors). Ice fishing is allowed in these four areas only. Regulations for fishing on the Northern lakes and Lake Defiance are posted at the site.

Various children's playground equipment and 11 miles of bicycle/hiking trails are also found within the park. The trails are open to cross-country skiers in the winter, and ice skating and sledding are permitted on Lake Defiance. For more information about Moraine Hills, contact Site Superintendent, 914 S. River Road, McHenry, Illinois 60050, phone 815/385-1624.

Chain O'Lakes State Park

Chain O'Lakes State Park, in northeastern Illinois, is in McHenry and Lake counties 20 miles west of Lake Michigan and four miles south of the Illinois-Wisconsin border. The 1,541-acre park and the 3,230-acre

139

Chain O'Lakes State Park

conservation area are primarily water and marshland. The area contains Illinois's largest concentration of natural lakes. The state park borders three of the ten lakes in the Fox Chain O'Lakes—Grass, Marie and Bluff.

Several picnic areas—with tables, outdoor stoves, water and toilets—are scattered throughout the park. There is also a pavilion, various playground equipment, and a concession stand that offers a variety of refreshments.

Fishing is popular around the river and lake banks within the park. Boat rentals, docks, fishing piers, and two launching ramps are also provided. There is no limit on motor size. Ice fishing and skating are permitted, dependent on ice thickness. Pheasants may be hunted, by permit only, in the conservation area adjoining the park. During the hunting season, the park is closed for other activities.

There are seven tent or trailer camping areas, each with its own picnic area and modern shower building. A limited amount of electricity and two sanitary stations are available for trailer units. The Oak Point campground on the Fox River has free boat launching ramps. Group camping is also available; groups of over 25 persons must have advance permission to enter the park. All campers must secure a permit from the park staff.

For additional information about the Chain O'Lakes State Park, contact Ranger, R.R.1, Box 423A, Spring Grove, 60081, phone 312/587-5512.

Illinois Beach State Park

Located between Waukegan and Zion in Lake County, Illinois Beach State Park occupies 3.5 miles of Lake Michigan shoreline. The 1,917-acre park offers a variety of uses: a general recreation area in the north portion of the park, a nature study area between Beach Road and Dead River, and a nature preserve south of Dead River. The Lake Michigan dunes that run through the park contain the only natural beach and dune association in Illinois.

A camping permit must be obtained from the park ranger to use either the tent camping sites or the trailer pads, many of which have electric service. Showers and flush toilets can be found in the utility building, which also has facilities to accommodate the physically handicapped. A sanitary dump station is nearby.

Swimming along the lake shoreline is permitted during the summer season, with lifeguards on duty from 10 a.m. to 8 p.m. Four beach houses provide hot showers, flush toilets, and dressing rooms; Beach

House No. 4 contains a camper store as well as a souvenir and gift shop. A children's playground area is also on the beach. Fishing is prohibited except in designated ponds within the park.

Illinois Beach also offers a number of designated trails, with guided nature hikes regularly scheduled throughout the year. Picnickers can find many shaded areas complete with tables and stoves. No firewood or charcoal is provided by the park.

For an extended, more luxurious visit, the 106-room Illinois Beach Lodge is located near the shore next to the Nature Center. Each room is equipped with a color television, air conditioning, sliding glass door, and private terrace. There are dining facilities for small or large groups, parties, or private conferences. The lodge also has a snack bar, a game room, a souvenir and gift shop, an all-season olympic pool (with a children's wading pool and locker/shower rooms), tennis courts, and shuffleboard courts. Near the park is an 18-hole golf course.

For further information about the park, contact the site manager, Illinois Beach State Park, Zion, Illinois 60099 (telephone: 312/662-4811). For information concerning the lodge, call 312/244-2000.

MUSEUMS OF THE CHICAGO AREA

After exercising your body and taking some time to appreciate the wonders of nature, why not explore your heritage or follow up on a particular interest? The museums and other such fascinating places listed hereafter cover a wide variety of tastes and all of them are quite inexpensive, making them ideal for family outings.

The admission prices listed here are the most recent available. However, since prices have fluctuated lately, it would be wise for the strict-budgeting individual to call ahead for verification of admission fees. Certain museums can be visited by reservation only or by appointment; they have been noted accordingly. Also, several museums conduct special classes for interested parties, ranging from furniture reupholstery to telescope making. These programs usually are related to the theme of the museums, and their staffs will be pleased to provide you with further information. Unless specified, all telephone numbers have the area code (312).

The museums marked with an asterisk (*) are described in detail along with stunning full-color photographs in the book, *Museums of Chicago*, also compiled by Museum Publications of America.

MAJOR LAKEFRONT MUSEUMS

Adler Planetarium
1300 S. Lake Shore Drive,
Chicago; 322-0300 & 0304
Admission: Free every day.
Hours: 6/16-8/31 9: 30-9;
9/1-6/15 MTWTh 9: 30-4: 30,
F 9: 30-9: 00, St Sn & hols. 9: 30-
5. *Sky Show:* $.75-1.50, seniors
free. Hours: M-Th at 2; F at 2 and
8: 00; St, Sn & hols at 11, 1, 2, 3,
and 4.

Art Institute of Chicago
Michigan Ave. at Adams;
443-3500.
Admission: Free, Th 10: 30-8;
discretionary fee MTWF
10: 30-4: 30, St 10-5, Sn & hols.
12-5.

Chicago Academy of Sciences
2001 N. Clark; 549-0606.
Admission: Free, 10-5 daily
(except Christmas).

Chicago Public Library Cultural Center
78 W. Washington; 269-2387.
Admission: Free, m-Th 9-9, F 9-5,
St 9-5.

Field Museum of Natural History
S. Lake Shore Drive & Roosevelt
Road (1200 South); 922-9410.
Admission: Free F 9-9; $1.50
MTWThStSn 9-5.

Chicago Historical Society
Clark & North; 642-4600.
Admission: Free, M 9: 30-
4: 30; $1.00 TWThFSt 9: 30-4: 30,
Sn and hols. 12-5.

Museum of Contemporary Art
237 E. Ontario; 943-7755.
Admission: $.50-1.00, MTWFSt
10-5, Sn 12-5.

Museum of Science and Industry
East 57th & Lake Shore Drive;
684-1414.
Admission: Free, M-F 9: 30-4,
St Sn & hols. 9: 30-5: 30.

ETHNIC MUSEUMS IN CHICAGO

Balzekas Museum of Lithuanian Culture
4012 S. Archer; 847-2441.
Admission: $.50-1.00, daily 1-4.

DuSable Museum of African-American History
57th And Cottage Grove (in
Washington Park); 947-0600.
Admission: 25-50 c, M-F 9-5,
St Sn 1-5.

Polish Museum
984 Milwaukee Ave.; 384-3352.
Admission; Free, daily 1-4.

Maurice Spertus Museum of Judaica
618 S. Michigan Ave.; 922-9012.
Admission: Free, F 10-3; $1.00
M-Th 10-5, Sn 10-3.

Ukranian Institute of Modern Art
2247 W. Chicago Ave.; 235-8255.
Admission: Free, F 7 p.m.-9 p.m.,
St 11-3, Sn 12-3 or by appt.

Ukranian National Museum
2453 W. Chicago Ave.; 276-6565.
Admission: Free, Sn 12-3 or by
appt.

Morton B. Weiss Museum of Judaica
KAM Tsaiah Israel Congregation,
1100 E. Hyde Park; 924-1234.
Admission: Free, M-F 9-4: 30.
—Excellent collection of Iranian
Judaica.

LOCAL HERITAGE MUSEUMS

Arlington Heights Historical Museum
500 N. Vail, Arlington Heights, Ill.; 255-1225.
Admission: 25-50c, W 2-4, St 1-4, Sn 2-5. Museum Country Store (c. 1893): Th-St 1-4.

Aurora Historical Museum
304 Oak Ave., Aurora, Ill.; 897-902..
Admission: Free (10c and 25c charge for groups) W-Sn 2-4: 30.

Barrington Historical Society
111 W. Station, Barrington, Ill.; 381-1730 or 381-4224.
Admission: Free W 10-12 noon, Th 1-4, Sn 2-4.

Czechoslovak Society of America Museum
2701 Harlem Ave., Berwyn, Ill.; 795-5800.
Admission: Free, MWF 9-4: 30.
—a history of the Czech and Slovak people in the Chicago area.

Des Plaines Historical Soceity
777 Lee, Des Plaines, Ill.; 297-4912.
Admission: 25c, families 50c, WStSn 2-4.

DuPage County Historical Museum
102 E. Wesley St., Wheaton, Ill.; 682-7343.
Admission: Free MWFSt 10-4.

Ellwood House
509 N. First, DeKalb, Ill.; (815)
756-4609.
Admission: Free, SnMWFSt 2-4

Elmhurst Historical Commission
104 S. Kenilworth Ave., Elmhurst,
Ill.; 833-1457.
Admission: Free TWTh 1-5, St
10-5.

Evanston Historical Society
225 Greenwood (at Sheridan),
Evanston, Ill.; 475-3410.
Admission: Free, F 1-5; 50c,
families $1.00, MTTHSt 1-5.

Frank Lloyd Wright Home &
Studio Foundation
951 Chicago Ave., Oak Park, Ill.;
848-1978.
Admission: $2.00 TTh 1-3, St Sn
1-5. —walking tours available.

Geneva Historical Society Museum
Wheeler Park, Third and Stevens
Sts., Geneva, Ill.
Admission: Free, 2-4:30 or by
appt. Curator: Mary L. Wheeler, 41
S. Lincoln Ave., Geneva.

Graue Mill
York Rd., ½ mile north of Ogden
Ave., Hinsdale, Ill. ; 654-9703.
Admission: 10-50c, 10-5 daily.
—water-powered stone grain mill,
former underground railroad
"station," a rest stop for escaped
slaves fleeing to Canada.

LOCAL HERITAGE MUSEUMS

Highland Park Historical Society Museum
326 Central, Highland Park, Ill.;
432-7090.
Admission: Free, T-St 1: 30-5,
Sn 2-4.

Lemont Area Historical Museum
306 Lemont, Lemont, Ill.;
257-6308, 257-6922.
Admission: Free, Sn 1-4.
—built in 1861.

Lombard Historical Museum
23 W. Maple, Lombard, Ill.;
629-1885.
Admission: 25-50c, WSn 1-4.
—1870-style Victorian home.

Martin-Mitchell Museum
Century Memorial Chapel, 234 W.
Aurora, Naperville, Ill.; 355-0274.
Admission: Free, WSn & hols.
1: 30-4: 30.

Oak Park and River Forest Historical Society Museum Room
Pleasant & Home Aves., Oak Park,
Ill.; 386-6777.
Admission: Free, Sn 3-5.

Caspar Ott Log House
501 Deerfield Rd., Deerfield, Ill.;
945-5321.
Admission: Discretionary fee, 1st
and 3rd Sundays of each month
from 2-4.
—1837 home, the oldest in Lake
County.

Pilcher Park Nature Museum
Off U.S. 30 on E. side of Joliet,
Ill.; (815) 726-2207.
Admission: Free, daily 9-5, StSn
10-5
—restored French fort, nature
museum and trails.

Pullman Community
115th St., just west of the Calumet
Expressway in Chicago;
Admission: Free, tours available
first Sun of May-Oct.
—former company town built in
late 1800s. For additional
information, contact Illinois Labor
History Society, Box 914, Chicago,
IL 60690; 248-8700.

Will County Historical Society
803 S. State St., Lockport, Ill.;
(815) 838-5080.
Admission: Free, 1-4: 30 daily.

MUSEUMS & PLACES WITH A SPECIFIC THEME

Jane Addams's Hull House
Halsted and Polk, Chicago;
996-2793.
Admission: Free, M-F 10-4, Sn
1-5.
—Immigrant life in the neighbor-
hood and the history of the original
Hull House Settlement.

ArchiCenter
111 S. Dearborn, Chicago;
782-1776.
Admission: Free, T-F 9-6,
St. 9-5, Sn 1-5.
—Devoted to Chicago architecture.

Baha'i House of Worship
Sheridan and Linden, Wilmette;
256-4400.
Admission: Free, daily 10-10 5/15-
10/14; 10-5 10/15-5/14.

Cantigny
1S151 Winfield Rd., two miles
west of Wheaton, Ill.; 668-5161.
Admission: Free, 9-7:30 daily.
First Division Museum: 10/1-5/1,
T-Sn 10-4; 5/2-9/30, T-Sn 9-5.
House Museum: winter, W-Sn
12-4; summer, W-Sn 12-5.

Eugene A Cernan Space Center
Triton College, 2000 Fifth, River
Grove, Ill.; 456-5815.
Admission: $.50-1.00, families
$2.50, wkdys 9-5 & 5-7; St & Sn
Noon-12 midnight.

Chicago Historical Antique Automobile Museum
3200 Skokie Valley, Highland Park, Ill.; 433-4400.
Admission: $1.75-2.75, Sn-Th 9-6, FSt 9 am-12 midnight.

Robert Crown Center for Health Education
21 Salt Creek Lane, Hinsdale; 325-1900.
Admission: School year: M-F 9-5: 30, by appt. only. School Groups $.75-$1.00 per student, teachers free. Summer: 9-2 weekdays, $1.00 per person, $3.00 per family.
—School year rates to increase to $1.00-$1.25 effective 9/1/80.

Martin D'Arcy Gallery of Art
Loyola University, 6525 N. Sheridan, Chicago; 274-3000.
Admission: Free, M-F 12-4, TTh evenings 6: 30-9: 30, Sn 1-4.

Frankfort on the Main
Routes 30 and 45, Frankfort, Ill.; (815) 469-3356.
Admission: Free, T-Sn 11: 30-4: 30.
—1890 style town, 25 miles southwest of Chicago.

Glessner House
1800 S. Prairie, Chicago; 325-1393.
Admission: $2.00, guided tours only. Hours: TThSt 10-4, Sn 1-5.
—A restored house serves as a tribute to Chicago architects and furniture designers.

The Grainery
Frankfurt, Ill.; (815) 469-4000.
Admission: Free, T-Sn
11: 30-4: 30.
—shopping center housed in a
former feed store, cobblestone
streets, nickelodeons, and
player pianos.

Hillary S. Jurica
Memorial Biology Museum
Illinois Benedictine College, Lisle,
Ill.; 968-7270, ext. 208.
Admission: Free, W 1: 30-3: 30,
Sn 2-4; groups by appt. two weeks
advance notice required.
—minerals, fossils, flora and
fauna.

Lindheimer Astronomical
Research Center
Northwestern University, 2353
Sheridan, Evanston, Ill.; 492-7651.
Admission: Free, St 2-4.

Lizzadro Museum of Lapidary Art
220 Cottage Hill, Elmhurst, Ill.;
833-1616.
Admission: Free F 1-5; 25-50c
TWTh 1-5, St 10-5, Sn 1-5.
—Lapidary art and a vast collection
of semiprecious stones.

Long Grove Village
Route 83 or 53 north to Long Grove
Road, Long Grove, Ill.; 634-0888.
Admission: Free, M-F 10-4: 30, St
10-5, Sn 12-5.
—Recreation of 1840 Illinois town.

MUSEUMS AND PLACES WITH A SPECIFIC THEME

Morton Arboretum
Route 53 near the E-W Tollway in
Lisle, Ill.; 968-0074.
Admission: $1.00 daily 9-7.
—No picnics allowed on grounds.

**Museum of Surgical Sciences and
Hall of Fame**
1524 N. Lake Shore Drive, Chicago,
642-3632.
Admission: Free, T-Sn 10-4.
—History and development of
surgery.

Oriental Institute Museum
Breasted Hall, University of
Chicago, 1155 E. 58th; 753-2474.
Admission: Free, T-St 10-4, Sn
12-4 (closed M, hols.)
—Ancient relics from the Near
East.

Perry Mastodon
Deicke Hall, Science Bldg.,
Wheaton College, Wheaton, Ill.;
682-5063.
Admission: Free, daily 7 a.m.-
10 p.m.
—Recorded lecture accompanies
fossil display.

Royal London Wax Museum
1419 N. Wells, Chicago; 337-7787.
Admission: $.75-$1.75 SnMTWTh
12-10:30, FSt 12-midnight. (Group
rates available)

David and Alfred Smart Gallery
University of Chicago, 5550 S.
Greenwood; 753-2121.
Admission: Free, T-St 10-4, Sn
12-4.

St. John's Church
For information, write Arlene Thiel, 5223 N. Hampshire Lane, McHenry, Ill. 60050; (815) 385-6451.

Admission: Closed until restoration is complete.
—Ongoing restoration of a German Gothic Church, to be completed in late 1979.

Stacy's Tavern
Main & Geneva, Glen Ellyn, Ill.; 858-8696.
Admission: Free, WFStSn 1-4.
—1846 tavern.

Svoboda's Nickelodeon Tavern
213 E. 24th St., Chicago Heights, Ill.; 758-0260.
Admission: Free, TWThFStSn, noon-1 a.m.
—149 antique musical devices play for a nominal fee (5c-50c)

The Olde Country Store
8420 Brookfield, Brookfield, Ill.
Admission: Free, StSn 11-5.
—1910 country store.

USS Silversides
Presently located at pier behind Naval Reserve Armory, at Monroe St., Chicago.